400TH ANNIVERSARY EDITION 1563-1963

the heidelberg catechism

UNITED CHURCH PRESS

Copyright 1962

UNITED CHURCH PRESS

This 400th Anniversary Edition of the Heidelberg Catechism is a translation from original German and Latin texts by Allen O. Miller and M. Eugene Osterhaven. The biblical quotations are from the *Revised Standard Version of the Bible* and from *The New English Bible, The New Testament*.

SECOND PRINTING 1963
THIRD PRINTING 1963
FOURTH PRINTING 1964
FIFTH PRINTING 1967
SIXTH PRINTING 1971
SEVENTH PRINTING 1973
EIGHTH PRINTING 1975
NINTH PRINTING 1976
TENTH PRINTING 1978
ELEVENTH PRINTING 1980

Library of Congress Catalog Card Number 62-20891
ISBN 0-8298-0060-3

United Church Press, 132 West 31 Street, New York, New York 10001

CONTENTS

FOREWORD AND INVITATION

The date January 19, 1963 marks the 400th anniversary of the Heidelberg Catechism. In behalf of the churches belonging to the North American Area of the World Alliance of Reformed and Presbyterian Churches, we are honored to present a new translation of this historic symbol of our catholic Christian faith, "reformed according to the Word of God."

The most ecumenical of the confessions of the Protestant Churches, the Heidelberg Catechism bears the name of the capital city of the German state in which it was written. The Reformation was introduced into the Palatinate in 1546, the year of Luther's death, and soon that region became a veritable battleground for various and contending evangelical views. Looking for advice, Frederick III, the wise prince who became Elector of this important principality in 1559, called upon a native son of the Palatinate, Philip Melanchthon, for assistance. Melanchthon counseled biblical simplicity, moderation, and peace as the gains of reform were being consolidated, and warned against extremes and scholastic subtleties in theological position. After a quarrel between two representatives of the Lutheran and Reformed parties at the altar of the Church of the Holy Spirit in Heidelberg, Frederick ordered a catechism to be written in an attempt to bring the people together.

The men chosen for this important task were Zacharias Ursinus and Caspar Olevianus, then twenty-eight and twenty-six years of age. Ursinus had been trained by Melanchthon and was a professor of theology at Heidelberg. Olevianus was a gifted biblical preacher. In the preparation of this catechism an earlier work of Ursinus, the *Catechesis Minor,* was used. Its three-fold division, based on the Epistle to the Romans, was taken over and about ninety of its questions were adopted with some modifications. A group of counselors, including the Elector, assisted the principal authors and revised parts of the work.

To Olevianus was given the responsibility for a final revision and translation into German. A man of eloquence, he was one "in whom imagination and pathos combined to clothe the logic of religion with beauty as well as power."

The publication of the Catechism in January, 1563 was a landmark in the German Reformation. According to the provisions of the Peace of Augsburg (1555) the Roman Catholic and Lutheran faiths were recognized, but "Zwinglian" or "Calvinist" views had no legal standing. The gradual reception of the Heidelberg Catechism by emperor, princes, and theologians makes a stirring story. The most significant event was the meeting of the Imperial Diet at Augsburg in the spring of 1566. Here, with the pomp that befitted the occasion, the Emperor read a decree charging the Elector Frederick with having introduced changes in the government and worship of the churches and a catechism dissenting from the Augsburg Confession.

Following a brief recess, the Elector reappeared accompanied by his son, John Casimir, his "spiritual armor-bearer," who carried the Bible and the Augsburg Confession. After a courageous defense reminiscent of Martin Luther's appearance before the Diet at Worms, Frederick, having won the admiration of the majority present, was judged as remaining within the teachings of the Augsburg Confession and to be a prince in good standing in the Empire. Thereafter the Heidelberg Catechism was more widely received and accepted by churches in other states and nations, and the praise accorded it probably exceeds that of any other statement of faith.

We are hopeful that this summary of evangelical teaching may, in our time, become a unitive confession not only for Lutheran and Reformed theologians, as it already was in the sixteenth century, but also for Congregational Christian and Evangelical and Reformed people in the United Church of Christ, for Presbyterian and Reformed Churches within the Alliance, and for an even wider fellowship of churches committed to the twentieth-century venture of reuniting the church, catholic, reformed, and evangelical.

We salute our predecessors, notably Philip Schaff and those who gave us the Tercentenary edition. Along with their very useful printing of the Catechism, with the German, Latin, and English versions in parallel columns, our primary resource has been Wilhelm Niesel's definitive German text, identifying first, second, and third editions, all from 1563, published in 1938. In order to show the biblical and theological precision of the Catechism, we have included in the present translation nearly all the biblical texts cited by the authors, using mainly the Revised Standard Version and occasionally the New

English Bible (N.E.B.). We have received the gracious and invaluable assistance of a score of scholars, both Presbyterian and Reformed, to whom we wish to make this public, though *incognito,* acknowledgment.

We invite the reader, both student and teacher, to enter as participants in the divine-human dialog of the drama of "man's redemption in Jesus Christ." The biblical covenant drama, as the outline for a catechism, was first recognized and taught by Martin Luther in his *Short Exposition* (1520):

"The Decalog teaches a man to know what is wrong with himself . . . to know himself to be a sinful and unrighteous man. Then the Creed shows and teaches him where to find the medicine, that is, divine grace . . . and the Lord's Prayer teaches him to yearn for this grace, to seek it and take it to heart."

This is the pattern which has become the trademark of the Heidelberg Catechism.

It is our conviction that one of the most significant uses of this Catechism, as we enter into the fifth century of its life, may be in adult education. We have therefore prepared a companion volume in which we offer a layman's commentary.

ALLEN O. MILLER,
   The United Church of Christ, *Chairman*
M. EUGENE OSTERHAVEN,
   The Reformed Church in America
ALADAR KOMJATHY,
   The Hungarian Reformed Church in America
JAMES I. McCORD,
   The World Alliance of Reformed Churches

1 / OUR ONLY COMFORT

❡ QUESTION 1. *What is your only comfort, in life and in death?*

That I belong—body and soul, in life and in death[a] —not to myself[b] but to my faithful Savior, Jesus Christ,[c] who at the cost of his own blood[d] has fully paid for all my sins[e] and has completely freed me from the dominion of the devil;[f] that he protects me so well[g] that without the will of my Father in heaven not a hair can fall from my head;[h] indeed, that everything must fit his purpose for my salvation.[i] Therefore, by his Holy Spirit, he also assures me of eternal life,[j] and makes me wholeheartedly willing and ready from now on to live for him.[k]

a. Rom. 14:8. If we live, we live to the Lord, and if we die, we die to the Lord; so then, whether we live or whether we die, we are the Lord's.
b. 1 Cor. 6:19-20. Do you not know that your body is a temple of the Holy Spirit within you, which you have from God? You are not your own; you were bought with a price.
c. 1 Cor. 3.23. You are Christ's; and Christ is God's.
d. 1 Peter 1:18-19. You know that you were ransomed . . . with the precious blood of Christ, like that of a lamb without blemish or spot.

9

e. 1 John 1:7; 2:2. If we walk in the light, as [God] is in the light, we have fellowship with one another, and the blood of Jesus his Son cleanses us from all sin. . . . He is the expiation for our sins, and not for ours only but also for the sins of the whole world.

f. 1 John 3:8. He who commits sin is of the devil; for the devil has sinned from the beginning. The reason the Son of God appeared was to destroy the works of the devil.
Cf. Heb. 2:14.

g. John 6:35, 39. Jesus said to them, . . . "This is the will of him who sent me, that I should lose nothing of all that he has given me, but raise it up at the last day."

h. Matt. 10:29-31. "Are not two sparrows sold for a penny? And not one of them will fall to the ground without your Father's will. But even the hairs of your head are all numbered. Fear not, therefore; you are of more value than many sparrows."
Cf. Luke 21:16-18.

i. Rom. 8:28. We know that in everything God works for good with those who love him, who are called according to his purpose.

j. 2 Cor. 1:21-22. It is God who . . . has put his seal upon us and given us his Spirit in our hearts as a guarantee.
Cf. 2 Cor. 5:5; Rom. 8:16; Eph. 1:14.

k. Rom. 8:14, 17. For all who are led by the Spirit of God are sons of God . . . and if children, then heirs . . . with Christ, provided we suffer with him in order that we may also be glorified with him.

⟨ QUESTION 2. *How many things must you know that you may live and die in the blessedness of this comfort?*

Three.[a] First, the greatness of my sin and wretchedness.[b] Second, how I am freed from all my sins and their wretched consequences.[c] Third, what gratitude I owe to God for such redemption.[d]

a. Titus 3:3-8. At one time we ourselves in our folly and obstinacy were all astray. We were slaves to passions and pleasures of every kind. Our days were passed in malice and envy; we were odious ourselves and we hated one another.

   But when the kindness and generosity of God our Savior dawned upon the world, then, not for any good deeds of our own, but because he was merciful, he saved us. . . . For he sent down the Spirit upon us plentifully through Jesus Christ our Savior, so that, justified by his grace, we might in hope become heirs to eternal life.

   Those who have come to believe in God should see that they engage in honorable occupations, which are not only honorable in themselves, but also useful to their fellow men (N.E.B.).

b. John 9:41. Jesus said to them, "If you were blind, you would have no guilt; but now that you say, 'We see,' your guilt remains."
   Cf. Rom. 1:18—3:20.

c. John 17:1-3. Jesus . . . lifted up his eyes to heaven and said, "Father, the hour has come; glorify thy Son that the Son may glorify thee, since thou hast given him power over all flesh, to give eternal life to all whom thou hast given him. And this is eternal life, that they know thee the only true God, and Jesus Christ whom thou hast sent."

Cf. Rom. 3:21—8:39; Phil. 2:5-11; Acts 10:34-43.

d. 1 Peter 2:9-10. You are a chosen race, a royal priest-hood, a holy nation, God's own people, that you may declare the wonderful deeds of him who called you out of darkness into his marvelous light. Once you were no people but now you are God's people; once you had not received mercy but now you have received mercy.

Cf. Rom. 12—14; Eph. 5:8-10.

PART I

Man's Sin and Guilt—The Law of God

2 / OUR HUMAN GUILT

LORD'S DAY 2

❡ QUESTION 3. *Where do you learn of your sin and its wretched consequences?*

From the Law of God.[a]

a. Rom. 3:20. No human being will be justified in [God's] sight by works of the law since through the law comes knowledge of sin.
   Cf. Rom 7:7-25.

❡ QUESTION 4. *What does the Law of God require of us?*

Jesus Christ teaches this in a summary in Matthew 22:37-40:

"YOU SHALL LOVE THE LORD YOUR GOD WITH ALL YOUR HEART, AND WITH ALL YOUR SOUL, AND WITH ALL YOUR MIND.[a] THIS IS THE GREAT AND FIRST COMMANDMENT. AND A SECOND IS LIKE IT, YOU SHALL LOVE YOUR NEIGHBOR AS YOURSELF.[b] ON THESE TWO

COMMANDMENTS DEPEND ALL THE LAW AND THE PROPHETS." (Cf. Luke 10:27.)

a. Cf. Deut. 6:5.
b. Cf. Lev. 19:18.

❡ QUESTION 5. *Can you keep all this perfectly?*

No,[a] for by nature I am prone to hate God and my neighbor.[b]

a. Rom. 3:10, 23. None is righteous, no, not one. . . . All have sinned and fall short of the glory of God. 1 John 1:8. If we say we have no sin, we deceive ourselves, and the truth is not in us.
b. Rom. 8:7. The mind that is set on the flesh is hostile to God; it does not submit to God's law, indeed it cannot.
  Cf. Eph. 2:1-3; Titus 3:3.

❡ QUESTION 6. *Did God create man evil and perverse like this?*

No.[a] On the contrary, God created man good and in his image,[b] that is, in true righteousness and holiness,[c] so that he might rightly know God his Creator, love him with his whole heart, and live with him in eternal blessedness, praising and glorifying him.[d]

a. Gen. 1:31. God saw everything that he had made, and behold, it was very good.

14

b. Gen. 1:27. God created man in his own image, in the image of God he created him; male and female he created them.
Cf. Gen. 2:7.

c. Eph. 4:24. Put on the new nature, created after the likeness of God in true righteousness and holiness.
Cf. Col. 3:10.

d. Rev. 21:3. I heard a great voice from the throne saying, "Behold, the dwelling of God is with men. He will dwell with them, and they shall be his people, and God himself will be with them."

❦ QUESTION 7.   *Where, then, does this corruption of human nature come from?*

From the fall and disobedience of our first parents, Adam and Eve, in the Garden of Eden;[a] whereby our human life is so poisoned[b] that we are all conceived and born in the state of sin.[c]

a. Gen. 3:1-6. The serpent was more subtle than any other wild creature that the Lord God had made. He said to the woman, "Did God say, 'You shall not eat of any tree of the garden'?" And the woman said to the serpent, "We may eat of the fruit of the trees of the garden; but God said, 'You shall not eat of the fruit of the tree which is in the midst of the garden, neither shall you touch it, lest you die.' " But the serpent said to the woman, "You will not die. For God knows that when you eat of it your eyes will be opened, and you will be like God, knowing good and evil." So when the woman

15

saw that the tree was good for food, and that it was a delight to the eyes, and that the tree was to be desired to make one wise, she took of its fruit and ate; and she also gave some to her husband, and he ate.

b. Rom. 5:12. As sin came into the world through one man and death through sin, . . . so death spread to all men because all men sinned.

c. Ps. 51:5. Behold, I was brought forth in iniquity, and in sin did my mother conceive me.

¶ QUESTION 8.   *But are we so perverted that we are altogether unable to do good and prone to do evil?*

Yes,[a] unless we are born again through the Spirit of God.[b]

a. Gen. 6:5. The Lord saw that the wickedness of man was great in the earth, and that every imagination of the thoughts of his heart was only evil continually.
Isa. 53:6. All we like sheep have gone astray; we have turned everyone to his own way.
Job. 14:4. Who can bring a clean thing out of an unclean? There is not one.
John 3:6. Jesus answered, . . . "That which is born of the flesh is flesh, and that which is born of the Spirit is spirit."

b. John 3:5. "Truly, truly, I say to you, unless one is born of water and the Spirit, he cannot enter the kingdom of God."

❡ QUESTION 9.   *Is not God unjust in requiring of man in his Law what he cannot do?*

No, for God so created man that he could do it.[a] But man, upon the instigation of the devil,[b] by deliberate disobedience, has cheated himself and all his descendants out of these gifts.[c]

a. Gen. 1:31. God saw everything that he had made, and behold, it was very good.

b. John 8:44. Jesus said to them, "You are of your father the devil, and your will is to do your father's desires. He was a murderer from the beginning, and has nothing to do with the truth, because there is no truth in him. When he lies, he speaks according to his own nature, for he is a liar and the father of lies."

c. Rom. 5:12, 18-19. As sin came into the world through one man and death through sin, . . . so death spread to all men because all men sinned. . . . One man's trespass led to condemnation for all men. . . . By one man's disobedience many were made sinners.
Cf. Gen. 3.

❡ QUESTION 10. *Will God let man get by with such disobedience and defection?*

Certainly not, for the wrath of God is revealed from heaven, both against our inborn sinfulness and our actual sins,[a] and he will punish them according to his righteous judgment in time and in eternity, as he has declared: "Cursed be everyone who does not abide by all things written in the book of the Law, and do them."[b]

a. Rom. 1:18. The wrath of God is revealed from heaven against all ungodliness and wickedness of men.

b. Gal. 3:10. All who rely on works of the law are under a curse; for it is written, "Cursed be every one who does not abide by all things written in the book of the law, and do them."

Cf. Deut. 27:26; 28:15.

❡ QUESTION 11. *But is not God also merciful?*

God is indeed merciful[a] and gracious, but he is also righteous.[b] It is his righteousness which requires that sin committed against the supreme majesty of God be punished with extreme, that is, with eternal punishment of body and soul.[c]

a. Exod. 34:6-7. The Lord passed before [Moses], and proclaimed, "The Lord, the Lord, a God merciful and gracious, slow to anger, and abounding in steadfast love and faithfulness, keeping steadfast love for thousands, forgiving iniquity and transgression and sin."

b. Exod. 20:5. "I the Lord your God am a jealous God, visiting the iniquity of the fathers upon the children to the third and the fourth generation of those who hate me."

Ps. 5:4-6. Thou art not a God who delights in wickedness; evil may not sojourn with thee. The boastful may not stand before thy eyes; thou hatest all evildoers. Thou destroyest those who speak lies; the Lord abhors bloodthirsty and deceitful men.

c. Matt. 25:45-46. Then [the King] will answer them, "Truly, I say to you, as you did it not to one of the least of these, you did it not to me." And they will go away into eternal punishment, but the righteous into eternal life.

PART II

Man's Redemption and Freedom—The Grace of God in Jesus Christ

---

4 / JUSTIFICATION BY GRACE

LORD'S DAY 5

❡ QUESTION 12. *Since, then, by the righteous judgment of God we have deserved temporal and eternal punishment, how may we escape this punishment, come again to grace, and be reconciled to God?*

God wills that his righteousness be satisfied;[a] therefore, payment in full must be made to his righteousness, either by ourselves or by another.[b]

a. Exod. 23:7. God said: "I will not acquit the wicked."
   Cf. Exod. 20:5; 34:7; Deut. 7:9-11.
b. Rom. 8:3-4. Sending his own Son in the likeness of sinful flesh and for sin, [God] condemned sin in the flesh, in order that the just requirement of the law might be fulfilled.

QUESTION 13. *Can we make this payment ourselves?*

By no means. On the contrary, we increase our debt each day.[a]

a. Job. 9:3. If one wished to contend with [God], one could not answer him once in a thousand times.
Rom. 2:4-5. Do you not know that God's kindness is meant to lead you to repentance? But by your hard and impenitent heart you are storing up wrath for yourself on the day of wrath when God's righteous judgment will be revealed.
Matt. 6:12. "Forgive us our debts, as we also have forgiven our debtors."

QUESTION 14. *Can any mere creature make the payment for us?*

No one. First of all, God does not want to punish any other creature for man's debt.[a] Moreover, no mere creature can bear the burden of God's eternal wrath against sin and redeem others from it.[b]

a. Ezek. 18:20. The soul that sins shall die.
Heb. 2:14-15. Since therefore the children share in flesh and blood, [Jesus] himself likewise partook of the same nature, that through death he might destroy him who has the power of death, that is, the devil, and deliver all those who through fear of death were subject to lifelong bondage.
b. Ps. 130:3. If thou, O Lord, shouldst mark iniquities, Lord, who could stand?

Ps. 49:7. Truly no man can ransom himself, or give to God the price of his life.

◖ QUESTION 15. *Then, what kind of mediator and redeemer must we seek?*

One who is a true[a] and righteous man[b] and yet more powerful than all creatures, that is, one who is at the same time true God.[c]

a. 1 Cor. 15:21. As by a man came death, by a man has come also the resurrection of the dead.

b. Isa. 53:9. They made his grave with the wicked and with a rich man in his death, although he had done no violence, and there was no deceit in his mouth.

Heb. 7:26. It was fitting that we should have such a high priest, holy, blameless, unstained, separated from sinners, exalted above the heavens.

2 Cor. 5:21. For our sake [God] made him to be sin who knew no sin, so that in him we might become the righteousness of God.

c. Isa. 9:6. To us a child is born, to us a son is given; and the government will be upon his shoulder, and his name will be called "Wonderful Counselor, Mighty God, Everlasting Father, Prince of Peace." Cf. Jer. 23:5-6.

❡ QUESTION 16. *Why must he be a true and righteous man?*

Because God's righteousness requires[a] that man who has sinned should make reparation for sin, but the man who is himself a sinner cannot pay for others.[b]

a. Rom. 5:12, 15. Sin came into the world through one man and death through sin . . . but the free gift is not like the trespass. For if many died through one man's trespass, much more have the grace of God and the free gift in the grace of that one man Jesus Christ abounded for many.
b. 1 Peter 3:18. Christ also died for sins once for all, the righteous for the unrighteous, that he might bring us to God, being put to death in the flesh but made alive in the Spirit.
    Cf. Isa. 53:3-5, 10-11.

❡ QUESTION 17. *Why must he at the same time be true God?*

So that by the power of his divinity he might bear as a man the burden of God's wrath,[a] and recover for us[b] and restore to us righteousness and life.[c]

a. Isa. 53:8. By oppression and judgment [the Lord's Servant] was taken away; and as for his generation, who considered that he was cut off out of the land of the living, stricken for the transgression of my people?

b. Acts 2:23-24. "This Jesus . . . you crucified and killed by the hands of lawless men. But God raised him up, having loosed the pangs of death, because it was not possible for him to be held by it."

John 1:4. In him was life, and the life was the light of men.

c. John 3:16. God so loved the world that he gave his only Son, that whoever believes in him should not perish but have eternal life.

2 Cor. 5:21. For our sake [God] made him to be sin who knew no sin, so that in him we might become the righteousness of God.

❑ QUESTION 18. *Who is this mediator who is at the same time true God and a true and perfectly righteous man?*

Our Lord Jesus Christ,[a] who is freely given to us for complete redemption and righteousness.[b]

a. Matt. 1:23. "Behold, a virgin shall conceive and bear a son, and his name shall be called Emmanuel" (which means, God with us).

Luke 2:11. "To you is born this day in the city of David a Savior, who is Christ the Lord."

Cf. 1 Tim. 3:16.

b. 1 Cor. 1:30. You are in Christ Jesus by God's act, for God has made him our wisdom; he is our righteousness; in him we are consecrated and set free (N.E.B.).

5 / THE HOLY TRINITY

❡ QUESTION 19. *Whence do you know this?*

From the holy gospel, which God himself revealed in the beginning in the Garden of Eden,[a] afterward proclaimed through the holy patriarchs[b] and prophets[c] and foreshadowed through the sacrifices and other rites of the Old Covenant,[d] and finally fulfilled through his own well-beloved Son.[e]

a. Gen. 3:14-15. The Lord God said to the serpent: "I will put enmity between you and the woman, and between your seed and her seed; he shall bruise your head, and you shall bruise his heel."

b. Gen. 22:18. "By your descendants shall all the nations of the earth bless themselves, because you have obeyed my voice."
   Gen. 49:10. "The sceptre shall not depart from Judah, nor the ruler's staff from between his feet, until he comes to whom it belongs; and to him shall be the obedience of the peoples."

c. Heb. 1:1-2. In many and various ways God spoke of old to our fathers by the prophets; but in these last days he has spoken to us by a Son, whom he appointed the heir of all things, through whom also he created the world.
   Acts 10:43. "To [Jesus of Nazareth] all the prophets bear witness that everyone who believes in him receives forgiveness of sins through his name."
   Cf. Rom. 1:1-6; Acts 3:22-26.

d. Heb. 9:13-15. If the sprinkling of defiled persons

25

with the blood of goats and bulls and with the ashes of a heifer sanctifies for the purification of the flesh, how much more shall the blood of Christ, who through the eternal Spirit offered himself without blemish to God, purify your conscience from dead works to serve the living God. Therefore he is the mediator of a new covenant.

Cf. Heb. 9:1—10:10.

e. Gal. 4:4-5. When the time had fully come, God sent forth his Son, born of woman, born under the law, to redeem those who were under the law, so that we might receive adoption as sons.

Cf. Rom. 10:4.

℟ QUESTION 20. *Will all men, then, be saved through Christ as they became lost through Adam?*

No. Only those who, by true faith, are incorporated into him and accept all his benefits.[a]

a. John 1:11-13. He came to his own home, and his own people received him not. But to all who received him, who believed in his name, he gave power to become children of God; who were born, not of blood nor of the will of the flesh nor of the will of man, but of God.

Rom. 11:17-20. If some of the branches were broken off, and you, a wild olive shoot, were grafted in their place to share the richness of the olive tree, do not boast over the branches. If you do boast, remember it is not you that support the root, but the root that supports you. You will say, "Branches were broken off so that I might be grafted in." That is true. They were broken off because of their unbelief, but you stand fast only through faith. So do not become proud, but stand in awe.

Heb. 4:2; 10:39. Good news came to us just as to them; but the message which they heard did not benefit them, because it did not meet with faith in the hearers. . . . But we are not of those who shrink back and are destroyed, but of those who have faith and keep their souls.

Cf. Isa. 53:11; Heb. 11.

❡ QUESTION 21. *What is true faith?*

It is not only a certain knowledge by which I accept as true all that God has revealed to us in his Word,[a] but also a wholehearted trust which the Holy Spirit creates in me[b] through the gospel,[c] that, not only to others, but to me also God has given the forgiveness of sins, everlasting righteousness and salvation, out of sheer grace solely for the sake of Christ's saving work.[d]

a. John 17:3. "This is eternal life, that they know thee the only true God, and Jesus Christ whom thou hast sent."
   Cf. James 1:18.

b. Rom. 4:13, 16. The promise to Abraham and his descendants, that they should inherit the world, did not come through the law but through the

27

righteousness of faith. . . . That is why it depends on faith, in order that the promise may rest on grace.

Matt. 16:15-17. Jesus said to them, "But who do you say that I am?" Simon Peter replied, "You are the Christ, the Son of the living God." And Jesus answered him, "Blessed are you, Simon Bar-Jona! For flesh and blood has not revealed this to you, but my Father who is in heaven."

2 Cor. 1:21-22. It is God who . . . has put his seal upon us and given us his Spirit in our hearts as a guarantee.

c. Rom. 1:16. I am not ashamed of the gospel: it is the power of God for salvation to everyone who has faith, to the Jew first and also to the Greek.

Rom. 10:17. Faith comes from what is heard, and what is heard comes by the preaching of Christ.

d. Rom. 3:21-26. Now the righteousness of God has been manifested apart from law, although the law and the prophets bear witness to it, the righteousness of God through faith in Jesus Christ for all who believe. For there is no distinction; since all have sinned and fall short of the glory of God, they are justified by his grace as a gift, through the redemption which is in Christ Jesus, whom God put forward as an expiation by his blood, to be received by faith. This was to show God's righteousness, because in his divine forbearance he had passed over former sins; it was to prove at the present time that he himself is righteous and that he justifies him who has faith in Jesus.

Cf. Eph. 2:4-9; Gal. 2:15-16.

¶ QUESTION 22. *What, then, must a Christian believe?*

All that is promised us in the gospel,[a] a summary of which is taught us in the articles of the Apostles' Creed, our universally acknowledged confession of faith.

a. John 20:31. These are written that you may believe that Jesus is the Christ, the Son of God, and that believing you may have life in his name.
   Cf. Matt. 28:18-20; Acts 10:34-43.

¶ QUESTION 23. *What are these articles?*

I BELIEVE IN GOD THE FATHER ALMIGHTY, MAKER OF HEAVEN AND EARTH;

AND IN JESUS CHRIST, HIS ONLY-BEGOTTEN SON, OUR LORD: WHO WAS CONCEIVED BY THE HOLY SPIRIT, BORN OF THE VIRGIN MARY; SUFFERED UNDER PONTIUS PILATE, WAS CRUCIFIED, DEAD, AND BURIED; HE DESCENDED INTO HELL, THE THIRD DAY HE ROSE AGAIN FROM THE DEAD; HE ASCENDED INTO HEAVEN AND SITS AT THE RIGHT HAND OF GOD THE FATHER ALMIGHTY; FROM THENCE HE SHALL COME TO JUDGE THE LIVING AND THE DEAD.

I BELIEVE IN THE HOLY SPIRIT; THE HOLY CATHOLIC CHURCH; THE COMMUNION OF SAINTS; THE FORGIVENESS OF SINS; THE RESURRECTION OF THE BODY; AND THE LIFE EVERLASTING.

❡ QUESTION 24. *How are these articles divided?*

Into three parts: The first concerns God *the Father* and our *creation;* the second, God *the Son* and our *redemption;* and the third, God *the Holy Spirit* and our *sanctification.*

❡ QUESTION 25. *Since there is only one Divine Being,*[a] *why do you speak of three, Father, Son, and Holy Spirit?*

Because God has thus revealed himself in his Word, that these three distinct Persons are the one, true, eternal God.[b]

a. Deut. 6:4. "Hear, O Israel: The Lord our God is one Lord."
b. Matt. 3:16-17. When Jesus was baptized, he went up immediately from the water, and behold, the heavens were opened and he saw the Spirit of God descending like a dove, and alighting on him; and lo, a voice from heaven, saying, "This is my beloved Son, with whom I am well pleased."
Cf. Matt. 28:19; 2 Cor. 13:14.

6 / GOD THE FATHER

❡ QUESTION 26.   *What do you believe when you say: "I believe in God the Father Almighty, Maker of heaven and earth"?*

That the eternal Father of our Lord Jesus Christ, who out of nothing created heaven and earth with all that is in them,[a] who also upholds and governs them by his eternal counsel and providence,[b] is for the sake of Christ his Son my God and my Father.[c] I trust in him so completely that I have no doubt that he will provide me with all things necessary for body and soul.[d] Moreover, whatever evil he sends upon me in this troubled life he will turn to my good,[e] for he is able to do it, being almighty God, and is determined to do it, being a faithful Father.[f]

a. Ps. 90:1-2. Lord, thou hast been our dwelling place in all generations. Before the mountains were brought forth, or ever thou hadst formed the earth and the world, from everlasting to everlasting thou art God.

Isa. 44:24. Thus says the Lord, your Redeemer, who formed you from the womb: "I am the Lord, who made all things, who stretched out the heavens alone, who spread out the earth by myself."

Cf. Gen. 1; John 1:1-5; Ps. 33:6.

b. Matt. 10:29. Are not two sparrows sold for a

31

penny? And not one of them will fall to the ground without your Father's will.

Cf. Ps. 104; Heb. 1:1-3.

c. Rom. 8:15-16. You have received the spirit of sonship. When we cry, "Abba! Father!" it is the Spirit himself bearing witness with our spirit that we are children of God.

Cf. John 1:12-13; Gal. 4:4-7.

d. Luke 12:22. [Jesus] said to his disciples, "Therefore I tell you, do not be anxious about your life, what you shall eat, nor about your body, what you shall put on."

Cf. Matt. 6:25-44.

e. Rom. 8:28. We know that in everything God works for good with those who love him, who are called according to his purpose.

f. Matt. 7:9-11. "What man of you, if his son asks him for a loaf, will give him a stone? Or if he asks for a fish, will give him a serpent? If you then, who are evil, know how to give good gifts to your children, how much more will your Father who is in heaven give good things to those who ask him?"

LORD'S DAY 10

℀ QUESTION 27. *What do you understand by the providence of God?*

The almighty and ever-present power of God[a] whereby he still upholds, as it were by his own hand, heaven and earth together with all creatures,[b] and rules in such a way that leaves and grass, rain and drought, fruitful and unfruitful years, food and drink,[c] health and sickness,[d] riches and poverty,[e] and everything else, come to us not by chance but by his fatherly hand.[f]

a. Acts 17:24-25. The God who made the world and everything in it, being Lord of heaven and earth, does not live in shrines made by man, nor is he served by human hands, as though he needed anything, since he himself gives to all men life and breath and everything.
Cf. Acts 17:26-28.

b. Heb. 1:3. He reflects the glory of God and bears the very stamp of his nature, upholding the universe by his word of power. When he had made purification for sins, he sat down at the right hand of the Majesty on high.

c. Acts 14:15-17. "You should turn from these vain things to a living God who made the heaven and the earth and the sea and all that is in them. In past generations he allowed all the nations to walk in their own ways; yet he did not leave himself without witness, for he did good and gave you from heaven rains and fruitful seasons, satisfying your hearts with good and gladness."
Cf. Jer. 5:24.

d. John 9:3. Jesus answered, "It was not that this man sinned, or his parents, but that the works of God might be made manifest in him."

e. Prov. 22:2. The rich and the poor meet together; the Lord is the maker of them all.
Cf. Matt. 10:29-31.

f. Eph. 1:11. In Christ indeed we have been given our share in the heritage, as was decreed in his design whose purpose is everywhere at work (N.E.B.).

❡ QUESTION 28. *What advantage comes from acknowledging God's creation and providence?*

We learn that we are to be patient in adversity,[a] grateful in the midst of blessing,[b] and to trust our faithful God and Father for the future, assured that no creature shall separate us from his love,[c] since all creatures are so completely in his hand that without his will they cannot even move.[d]

a. Rom. 5:3-4. We rejoice in our sufferings, knowing that suffering produces endurance, and endurance produces character, and character produces hope. Cf. James 1:3; Job 1:21.
b. Deut. 8:10. "You shall eat and be full, and you shall bless the Lord your God for the good land he has given you."
c. Rom. 8:38-39. I am sure that neither death, nor life, nor angels, nor principalities, nor things present, nor things to come, nor powers, nor height, nor depth, nor anything else in all creation, will be able to separate us from the love. of God in Christ Jesus our Lord.
d. Acts 17:28. "In him we live and move and have our being."
Cf. Acts 17:25; Job 1:12; Prov. 21:1.

7 / GOD THE SON

❡ QUESTION 29. *Why is the Son of God called* JESUS, *which means* SAVIOR?

Because he saves us from our sins,[a] and because salvation is to be sought or found in no other.[b]

a. Matt. 1:21. "She will bear a son, and you shall call his name Jesus, for he will save his people from their sins."
   Cf. Heb. 7:25.
b. Acts 4:12. "There is salvation in no one else, for there is no other name under heaven given among men by which we must be saved."

❡ QUESTION 30. *Do those who seek their salvation and well-being from saints, by their own efforts, or by other means really believe in the only Savior Jesus?*

No. Rather, by such actions they deny Jesus, the only Savior and Redeemer, even though they boast of belonging to him.[a] It therefore follows that either Jesus is not a perfect Savior, or those who receive this Savior with true faith must possess in him all that is necessary for their salvation.[b]

a. 1 Cor. 1:12-13. Each one of you says, "I belong to Paul," or "I belong to Apollos," or "I belong to Cephas," or "I belong to Christ." Is Christ divided?

Was Paul crucified for you? Or were you baptized in the name of Paul?

Cf. Gal. 5:4.

b. Col. 1:19-20. In him all the fullness of God was pleased to dwell, and through him to reconcile to himself all things, whether on earth or in heaven, making peace by the blood of his cross.

Cf. Isa. 9:6-7; John 1:16.

❡ QUESTION 31. *Why is he called* CHRIST, *that is, the* ANOINTED ONE?

Because he is ordained by God the Father and anointed with the Holy Spirit[a] to be *our chief Prophet* and *Teacher*,[b] fully revealing to us the secret purpose and will of God concerning our redemption;[c] to be *our only High Priest*,[d] having redeemed us by the one sacrifice of his body and ever interceding for us with the Father;[e] and to be *our eternal King*, governing us by his Word and Spirit, and defending and sustaining us in the redemption he has won for us.[f]

a. Luke 3:21-22. When all the people were baptized, and when Jesus also had been baptized and was praying, the heaven was opened, and the Holy Spirit descended upon him in bodily form, as a dove, and a voice came from heaven, "Thou art my beloved Son; with thee I am well pleased."

Cf. Luke 4:14-19 (Isa. 61:1-2) ; Heb. 1:9.

b. Acts 3:22. "Moses said, 'The Lord God will raise up for you a prophet from your brethren as he raised me up. You shall listen to him in whatever he tells you.' "
Cf. Deut. 18:15, 18.

c. John 1:18. No one has ever seen God; the only Son, who is in the bosom of the Father, he has made him known.
Cf. John 15:15.

d. Heb. 7:17. It is witnessed of him, "Thou art a priest forever, after the order of Melchizedek."

e. Heb. 9:12, 28. He entered once for all into the Holy Place, taking not the blood of goats and calves but his own blood, thus securing an eternal redemption. . . . Christ, having been offered once to bear the sins of many, will appear a second time, not to deal with sin but to save those who are eagerly waiting for him.
Rom. 8:34. Is it Christ Jesus, who died, yes, who was raised from the dead, who is at the right hand of God, who indeed intercedes for us?

f. Luke 1:32-33. He will be great, and will be called the Son of the Most High; and the Lord God will give to him the throne of his father David, and he will reign over the house of Jacob forever; and of his kingdom there will be no end.
Zech. 9:9. Rejoice greatly, O daughter of Zion! Shout aloud, O daughter of Jerusalem! Lo, your king comes to you; triumphant and victorious is he, humble and riding on an ass, on a colt the foal of an ass.
Cf. Mark 11:1-10; Matt. 21:1-11.

Matt. 28:18. Jesus came and said to them, "All authority in heaven and on earth has been given to me."

(QUESTION 32. *But why are you called a Christian?*

Because through faith I share in Christ[a] and thus in his anointing,[b] so that I may confess his name,[c] offer myself a living sacrifice of gratitude to him,[d] and fight against sin and the devil with a free and good conscience throughout this life[e] and hereafter rule with him in eternity over all creatures.[f]

a. Acts 11:26. In Antioch the disciples were for the first time called Christians.

1 Cor. 12:27. You are the body of Christ and individually members of it.

b. Acts 2:17. "And in the last days it shall be, God declares, that I will pour out my Spirit upon all flesh, and your sons and your daughters shall prophesy, and your young men shall see visions, and your old men shall dream dreams."

Cf. Joel 2:28; 1 John 2:27.

c. Matt. 10:5, 32. These twelve Jesus sent out, charging them, . . . "Everyone who acknowledges me before men, I also will acknowledge before my Father who is in heaven."

d. Rom. 12:1. I appeal to you therefore, brethren, by the mercies of God, to present your bodies as a living sacrifice, holy and acceptable to God, which is your spiritual worship.

1 Peter 2:5, 9. Like living stones be yourselves built into a spiritual house, to be a holy priesthood, to offer spiritual sacrifices acceptable to God through Jesus Christ. . . . You are a chosen race, a royal priesthood, a holy nation, God's own people, that you may declare the wonderful deeds of him who called you out of darkness into his marvelous light.

e. 1 Tim. 1:18-19. Inspired by [prophetic utterances] you may wage the good warfare, holding faith and a good conscience.

f. 2 Tim. 2:11-13. The saying is sure: If we have died with him, we shall also live with him; if we endure, we shall also reign with him; if we deny him, he also will deny us; if we are faithless, he remains faithful—for he cannot deny himself.

LORD'S DAY 13

℃ QUESTION 33. *Why is he called* GOD'S ONLY-BEGOTTEN SON, *since we also are God's children?*

Because Christ alone is God's own eternal Son,[a] whereas we are accepted for his sake as children of God by grace.[b]

a. John 1:1-3, 14, 18. In the beginning was the Word, and the Word was with God, and the Word was God. He was in the beginning with God; all things were made through him, and without him was not anything made that was made. . . . The Word became flesh and dwelt among us, full of grace and truth; we have beheld his glory, glory as of the

only Son from the Father. . . . No one has ever
seen God; the only Son, who is in the bosom of
the Father, he has made him known.

Cf. Heb. 1:2.

b. Eph. 1:5-6. He destined us in love to be his sons
through Jesus Christ, according to the purpose of
his will, to the praise of his glorious grace which
he freely bestowed on us in the Beloved.

Cf. John 1:12; Rom. 8:15-17.

❡ QUESTION 34. *Why do you call him* OUR LORD?

Because, not with gold or silver but at the cost of
his blood,[a] he has redeemed us body and soul from
sin and all the dominion of the devil, and has
bought us for his very own.[b]

a. 1 Peter 1:18-19. You know that you were ransomed
from the futile ways inherited from your fathers,
not with perishable things such as silver or gold,
but with the precious blood of Christ, like that of
a lamb without blemish or spot.

Cf. 1 Peter 2:9-10.

b. 1 Cor. 7:23. You were bought with a price; do not
become slaves of men.

Cf. 1 Cor. 6:20.

❆ QUESTION 35. *What is the meaning of: "Conceived by the Holy Spirit, born
of the Virgin Mary"?*

That the eternal Son of God, who is and remains
true and eternal God,[a] took upon himself our true
manhood from the flesh and blood of the Virgin
Mary[b] through the action of the Holy Spirit,[c] so
that he might also be the true seed of David,[d] like
his fellow men in all things,[e] except for sin.[f]

a. John 1:1. In the beginning was the Word, and the
Word was with God, and the Word was God.
b. John 1:14. The Word became flesh and dwelt
among us, full of grace and truth; we have beheld
his glory, glory as of the only Son from the Father.
Cf. Gal. 4:4.
c. Luke 1:35. The angel said to her, "The Holy Spirit
will come upon you, and the power of the Most
High will overshadow you; therefore the child to
be born will be called holy, the Son of God."
Cf. Matt. 1:18, 20.
d. Rom. 1:1-3. The gospel of God [is] . . . the gospel
concerning his Son, who was descended from David
according to the flesh.
Cf. Ps. 132:11; 2 Sam. 7:12-17.
e. Phil. 2:5-7. Christ Jesus . . . emptied himself, taking the form of a servant, being born in the likeness of men.
f. Heb. 4:15. We have not a high priest who is unable to sympathize with our weaknesses, but one

who in every respect has been tempted as we are,
yet without sinning.

◀ QUESTION 36. *What benefit do you receive
from the holy conception and
birth of Christ?*

That he is our Mediator,[a] and that, in God's sight,
he covers over with his innocence and perfect holiness the sinfulness in which I have been conceived.[b]

a. 1 Tim. 2:5-6. There is one God, and there is one
    mediator between God and men, the man Christ
    Jesus, who gave himself as a ransom for all.
b. Rom. 4:7. Blessed are those whose iniquities are
    forgiven, and whose sins are covered.
    Cf. Ps. 32:1; 1 Cor. 1:30.

LORD'S DAY 15

◀ QUESTION 37. *What do you understand by the
word "suffered"?*

That throughout his life on earth, but especially
at the end of it, he bore in body and soul the wrath
of God against the sin of the whole human race,[a]
so that by his suffering, as the only expiatory sacrifice, he might redeem our body and soul from everlasting damnation, and might obtain for us God's
grace, righteousness, and eternal life.[b]

a. Isa. 53:12. He poured out his soul to death, and
    was numbered with the transgressors; yet he bore

the sin of many, and made intercession for the transgressors.

1 Peter 2:24. He himself bore our sins in his body on the tree, that we might die to sin and live to righteousness. By his wounds you have been healed.

b. Rom. 3:24-25. They are justified by his grace as a gift, through the redemption which is in Christ Jesus, whom God put forward as an expiation by his blood, to be received by faith. This was to show God's righteousness, because in his divine forbearance he had passed over former sins.
Cf. 1 John 2:2.

❡ QUESTION 38. *Why did he suffer "under Pontius Pilate" as his judge?*

That he, being innocent, might be condemned by an earthly judge,[a] and thereby set us free from the judgment of God which, in all its severity, ought to fall upon us.[b]

a. John 19:13-16. Pilate . . . brought Jesus out and sat down on the judgment seat at a place called The Pavement, and in Hebrew, Gabbatha. Now it was the day of Preparation for the Passover; it was about the sixth hour. He said to the Jews, "Here is your King!" They cried out, "Away with him, away with him, crucify him!" Pilate said to them, "Shall I crucify your King?" The chief priests answered, "We have no king but Caesar." Then he handed him over to them to be crucified.
Cf. Luke 23:13-24; Acts 4:27-28.

b. Isa. 53:4-5. Surely he has borne our griefs and carried our sorrows; yet we esteemed him stricken, smitten by God, and afflicted. But he was wounded for our transgressions, he was bruised for our iniquities; upon him was the chastisement that made us whole, and with his stripes we are healed.

Rom. 5:6. While we were yet helpless, at the right time Christ died for the ungodly.

Cf. 2 Cor. 5:21; Gal. 3:13.

❡ QUESTION 39. *Is there something more in his having been crucified than if he had died some other death?*

Yes, for by this I am assured that he took upon himself the curse which lay upon me, because the death of the cross was cursed by God.[a]

a. Gal. 3:13. Christ redeemed us from the curse of the law, having become a curse for us—for it is written, "Cursed be everyone who hangs on a tree." Cf. Deut. 21:23.

LORD'S DAY 16

❡ QUESTION 40. *Why did Christ have to suffer "death"?*

Because the righteousness and truth of God are such that nothing else could make reparation for our sins except the death of the Son of God.[a]

a. Heb. 2:9. We see Jesus, who for a little while was made lower than the angels, crowned with glory and honor because of the suffering of death, so that by the grace of God he might taste death for everyone.

Cf. Rom. 8:3-4.

❧ QUESTION 41. *Why was he "buried"?*

To confirm the fact that he was really dead.[a]

a. Acts 13:29. When they had fulfilled all that was written of him, they took him down from the tree, and laid him in a tomb.

Cf. Matt. 27:59-60; Luke 23:50-55; John 19:38-42.

❧ QUESTION 42. *Since, then, Christ died for us, why must we also die?*

Our death is not a reparation for our sins,[a] but only a dying to sin and an entering into eternal life.[b]

a. Rom. 7:24. Wretched man that I am! Who will deliver me from this body of death?

Ps. 49:7. Truly no man can ransom himself, or give to God the price of his life.

b. 1 Thess. 5:9-10. Our Lord Jesus Christ . . . died for us so that whether we wake or sleep we might live with him.

Cf. John 5:24.

❧ QUESTION 43. *What further benefit do we receive from the sacrifice and death of Christ on the cross?*

That by his power our old self is crucified, put to death, and buried with him,[a] so that the evil passions of our mortal bodies may reign in us no more,[b] but that we may offer ourselves to him as a sacrifice of thanksgiving.[c]

a. Rom. 6:6. We know that our old self was crucified with him so that the sinful body might be destroyed, and we might no longer be enslaved to sin. Cf. Col. 2:12.

b. Rom. 6:12. Let not sin therefore reign in your mortal bodies, to make you obey their passions.

c. Rom. 12:1. I appeal to you therefore, brethren, by the mercies of God, to present your bodies as a living sacrifice, holy and acceptable to God, which is your spiritual worship.

❧ QUESTION 44. *Why is there added: "He descended into hell"?*

That in my severest tribulations I may be assured that Christ my Lord has redeemed me from hellish anxieties and torment by the unspeakable anguish, pains, and terrors which he suffered in his soul both on the cross and before.[a]

a. Isa. 53:5. He was wounded for our transgressions, he was bruised for our iniquities; upon him was the chastisement that made us whole, and with his stripes we are healed.

Matt. 27:46. About the ninth hour Jesus cried with a loud voice, "Eli, Eli, lama sabach-thani?" that is, "My God, my God, why hast thou forsaken me?"

❧ QUESTION 45. *What benefit do we receive from "the resurrection" of Christ?*

First, by his resurrection he has overcome death that he might make us share in the righteousness which he has obtained for us through his death.[a] Second, we too are now raised by his power to a new life.[b] Third, the resurrection of Christ is a sure pledge to us of our blessed resurrection.[c]

a. Rom. 4:24-25. It will be reckoned [as righteousness] to us who believe in him that raised from the dead Jesus our Lord, who was put to death for our trespasses and raised for our justification.
   Cf. Heb. 2:14-15; 1 Peter 1:3, 21.
b. Rom. 6:3-4. Do you not know that all of us who have been baptized into Christ Jesus were baptized into his death? We were buried therefore with him by baptism into death, so that as Christ was raised from the dead by the glory of the Father, we too might walk in newness of life.
   Cf. Col. 3:1-5; Eph. 2:4-6.
c. Rom. 8:11. If the Spirit of him who raised Jesus from the dead dwells in you, he who raised Christ Jesus from the dead will give life to your mortal

bodies also through his Spirit which dwells in you.
Cf. 1 Cor. 15.

❰ QUESTION 46. *How do you understand the words: "He ascended into heaven"?*

That Christ was taken up from the earth into heaven before the eyes of his disciples[a] and remains there on our behalf[b] until he comes again to judge the living and the dead.[c]

a. Luke 24:50-51. [Jesus] led them out as far as Bethany, and lifting up his hands he blessed them. While he blessed them, he parted from them.
Cf. Acts 1:9.

b. Heb. 9:24. Christ has entered, not into a sanctuary made with hands, a copy of the true one, but into heaven itself, now to appear in the presence of God on our behalf.
Cf. Rom. 8:34; Eph. 4:8.

c. Acts 1:11. "Men of Galilee, why do you stand looking into heaven? This Jesus, who was taken up from you into heaven, will come in the same way as you saw him go into heaven."
Acts 10:42. He commanded us to preach to the people, and to testify that he is the one ordained by God to be judge of the living and the dead.
Cf. Matt. 25:31-46.

❡ QUESTION 47. *Then, is not Christ with us unto the end of the world, as he has promised us?*[a]

Christ is true man and true God. As a man **he is** no longer on earth,[b] but in his divinity, majesty, grace, and Spirit, he is never absent from us.[c]

a. Matt. 28:20. "Lo, I am with you always, to the close of the age."

b. John 17:11. "Now I am no more in the world, but they are in the world, and I am coming to thee. Holy Father, keep them in thy name which thou hast given me, that they may be one, even as we are one."
   Cf. John 16:28.

c. John 14:18-19. "I will not leave you desolate; I will come to you. Yet a little while, and the world will see me no more, but you will see me; because I live, you will live also."

❡ QUESTION 48. *But are not the two natures in Christ separated from each other in this way, if the humanity is not wherever the divinity is?*

Not at all; for since divinity is incomprehensible and everywhere present,[a] it must follow that the divinity is indeed beyond the bounds of the humanity which it has assumed, and is nonetheless ever in that humanity as well, and remains personally united to it.[b]

a. Jer. 23:23-24. "Am I a God at hand, says the Lord, and not a God afar off? Can a man hide himself in secret places so that I cannot see him? says the Lord. Do I not fill heaven and earth? says the Lord."

   Cf. Ps. 139:7-10.

b. John 3:13. No one has ascended into heaven but he who descended from heaven, the Son of man.

   Col. 2:9. In [Christ] the whole fullness of deity dwells bodily.

❡ QUESTION 49. *What benefit do we receive from Christ's ascension into heaven?*

First, that he is our Advocate in the presence of his Father in heaven.[a] Second, that we have our flesh in heaven as a sure pledge that he, as the Head, will also take us, his members, up to himself.[b] Third, that he sends us his Spirit as a counterpledge[c] by whose power we seek what is above, where Christ is, sitting at the right hand of God, and not things that are on earth.[d]

a. Rom. 8:34. Is it Christ Jesus, who died, yes, who was raised from the dead, who is at the right hand of God, who indeed intercedes for us?

   Cf. 1 John 2:1.

b. John 14:2. "In my Father's house are many rooms; if it were not so, would I have told you that I go to prepare a place for you?"

   Cf. John 17:24; 20:17.

c. John 14:16-17. "I will pray the Father, and he will give you another Counselor, to be with you forever, even the Spirit of truth."
Cf. Acts 2; 2 Cor. 1:22; 5:5.

d. Col. 3:1. You have been raised with Christ, seek the things that are above, where Christ is, seated at the right hand of God.
Cf. Phil. 3:20.

❡ QUESTION 50. *Why is there added: "And sits at the right hand of God"?*

Because Christ ascended into heaven so that he might manifest himself there as the Head of his Church,[a] through whom the Father governs all things.[b]

a. Eph. 1:20-23. [God] raised [Christ] from the dead and made him sit at his right hand in the heavenly places, far above all rule and authority and power and dominion, and above every name that is named, not only in this age but also in that which is to come; and he has put all things under his feet and has made him the head over all things for the church, which is his body, the fullness of him who fills all in all.
Cf. Col. 1:18.

b. Matt. 28:18. Jesus came and said to them, "All authority in heaven and on earth has been given to me."
Cf. John 5:22.

ℂ QUESTION 51. *What benefit do we receive from this glory of Christ, our Head?*

First, that through his Holy Spirit he pours out heavenly gifts upon us, his members.[a] Second, that by his power he defends and supports us against all our enemies.[b]

a. Acts. 2:33. Being therefore exalted at the right hand of God, and having received from the Father the promise of the Holy Spirit, he has poured out this which you see and hear.
Eph. 4:8. "When he ascended on high he led a host of captives, and he gave gifts to men."
b. John 10:28. "I give them eternal life, and they shall never perish, and no one shall snatch them out of my hand."

ℂ QUESTION 52. *What comfort does the return of Christ "to judge the living and the dead" give you?*

That in all affliction and persecution I may await with head held high the very Judge from heaven who has already submitted himself to the judgment of God for me and has removed all the curse from me;[a] that he will cast all his enemies and mine into everlasting condemnation,[b] but he shall take me, together with all his elect, to himself into heavenly joy and glory.[c]

a. Luke 21:28. "When these things begin to take place, look up and raise your heads, because your redemption is drawing near."

Phil. 3:20. Our commonwealth is in heaven, and from it we await a Savior, the Lord Jesus Christ.

b. Matt. 25:41-43. "He will say to those at his left hand, 'Depart from me, you cursed, into the eternal fire prepared for the devil and his angels; for I was hungry and you gave me no food, I was thirsty and you gave me no drink, I was a stranger and you did not welcome me, naked and you did not clothe me, sick and in prison and you did not visit me.' "

c. Matt. 25:34. "The King will say to those at his right hand, 'Come, O blessed of my Father, inherit the kingdom prepared for you from the foundation of the world.' "

8 / GOD THE HOLY SPIRIT

LORD'S DAY 20

❡ QUESTION 53. *What do you believe concerning "the Holy Spirit"?*

First, that, with the Father and the Son, he is equally eternal God;[a] second, that God's Spirit is also given to me,[b] preparing me through a true faith to share in Christ and all his benefits,[c] that he comforts me[d] and will abide with me forever.[e]

a. Gen. 1:1-2. When God began to create the heavens and the earth, the earth was without form and void, and darkness was upon the face of the deep; and the Spirit of God was moving over the face of the waters.

John 4:24. God is Spirit, and those who worship him must worship in spirit and truth.

Cf. John 14:7-17; Acts 5:3-4.

b. Matt. 28:19. "Go therefore and make disciples of all nations, baptizing them in the name of the Father and of the Son and of the Holy Spirit."

1 Cor. 3:16. Do you not know that you are God's temple and that God's Spirit dwells in you?

Cf. 2 Cor. 1:22.

c. 1 Cor. 6:17, 19. He who is united to the Lord becomes one spirit with him. . . . Do you not know that your body is a temple of the Holy Spirit within you, which you have from God? You are not your own.

Cf. Gal. 4:6-7.

d. Acts. 9:31. The church throughout all Judea and Galilee and Samaria had peace and was built up; and walking in the fear of the Lord and in the comfort of the Holy Spirit it was multiplied.

e. John 14:16. "I will pray the Father, and he will give you another Counselor, to be with you forever."

LORD'S DAY 21

❰ QUESTION 54. *What do you believe concerning "the Holy Catholic Church"?*

I believe that, from the beginning to the end of the world, and from among the whole human race,[a] the Son of God,[b] by his Spirit and his Word,[c] gathers, protects, and preserves for himself, in the unity of the true faith,[d] a congregation chosen for eternal life. Moreover, I believe that I am and forever will remain a living member of it.[e]

a. Gen. 26:3b-4. "I will fulfill the oath which I swore to Abraham your father. I will multiply your descendants as the stars of heaven, and will give to your descendants all these lands; and by your descendants all the nations of the earth shall bless themselves."

Rev. 5:9. They sang a new song, saying, "Worthy art thou to take the scroll and to open its seals, for thou wast slain and by thy blood didst ransom men for God from every tribe and tongue and people and nation."

b. Col. 1:18. [Christ] is the head of the body, the church; he is the beginning, the first-born from the dead, that in everything he might be preeminent.

c. Isa. 59:21. "This is my covenant with them, says the Lord: my spirit which is upon you, and my words which I have put in your mouth, shall not depart out of your mouth, or out of the mouth of your children, or out of the mouth of your children's children, says the Lord, from this time forth and forevermore."

Cf. Rom. 1:16-18; 10:14-17.

d. Acts 13:47-48. The Lord has commanded us, saying, "I have set you to be a light for the Gentiles, that you may bring salvation to the uttermost parts of the earth." And when the Gentiles heard this, they were glad and glorified the word of God; and as many as were ordained to eternal life believed. Cf. Isa. 49:6.

Eph. 4:3-6. [Be] eager to maintain the unity of the Spirit in the bond of peace. There is one body and one Spirit, just as you were called to the one hope that belongs to your call, one Lord, one faith, one baptism, one God and Father of us all, who is above all and through all and in all.

Eph. 5:25-27. Christ loved the church and gave himself up for her, that he might sanctify her, having cleansed her by the washing of water with the word, that the church might be presented before him in splendor, without spot or wrinkle or any such thing, that she might be holy and without blemish.

e. John 10:28. "I give them eternal life, and they shall never perish, and no one shall snatch them out of my hand."

Cf. Rom. 8:29-39.

℄ QUESTION 55. *What do you understand by "the communion of saints"?*

First, that believers one and all, as partakers of the Lord Christ, and all his treasures and gifts, shall share in one fellowship.[a] Second, that each one ought to know that he is obliged to use his gifts freely and with joy for the benefit and welfare of other members.[b]

a. 1 Cor. 1:9. God is faithful, by whom you were called into the fellowship of his Son, Jesus Christ our Lord.

1 Cor. 12:4-7, 12-13. There are varieties of gifts, but the same Spirit; and there are varieties of service, but the same Lord; and there are varieties of working, but it is the same God who inspires them all in everyone. To each is given the manifestation of the Spirit for the common good. . . . For just as the body is one and has many members, and all the members of the body, though many, are one body, so it is with Christ. For by one Spirit we were all baptized into one body—Jews or Greeks, slaves or free—and all were made to drink of one Spirit.

b. 1 Cor. 12:14, 21, 26-27. The body does not consist of one member but of many. . . . The eye cannot say to the hand, "I have no need of you," nor again the head to the feet, "I have no need of you." . . . If one member suffers, all suffer together; if one member is honored, all rejoice together. Now you are the body of Christ and individually members of it.

1 Cor. 13:4-5. Love is patient and kind; love is not jealous or boastful; it is not arrogant or rude. Love does not insist on its own way; it is not irritable or resentful.

Cf. Phil. 2:1-11; 1 Cor. 12—13.

❡ QUESTION 56. *What do you believe concerning "the forgiveness of sins"?*

That, for the sake of Christ's reconciling work,[a] God will no more remember my sins or the sinfulness with which I have to struggle all my life long;[b] but that he graciously imparts to me the righteousness of Christ so that I may never come into condemnation.[c]

a. 2 Cor. 5:19, 21. God was in Christ reconciling the world to himself, not counting their trespasses against them, and entrusting to us the message of reconciliation. . . . For our sake he made him to be sin who knew no sin, so that in him we might become the righteousness of God.

Cf. 1 John 1:7; 2:2.

b. Jer. 31:34. "No longer shall each man teach his neighbor and each his brother, saying, 'Know the Lord,' for they shall all know me, from the least of them to the greatest, says the Lord; for I will forgive their iniquity, and I will remember their sin no more."

Cf. Ps. 103.

Rom. 8:1-2. There is therefore now no condemnation for those who are in Christ Jesus. For the law of the Spirit of life in Christ Jesus has set me free from the law of sin and death.

c. John 3:17-18. God sent the Son into the world, not to condemn the world, but that the world might be saved through him. He who believes in him is not condemned.

LORD'S DAY 22

❰ QUESTION 57. *What comfort does "the resurrection of the body" give you?*

That after this life my soul shall be immediately taken up to Christ, its Head,[a] and that this flesh of

58

mine, raised by the power of Christ, shall be re-united with my soul, and be conformed to the glorious body of Christ.[b]

a. Luke 23:43. [Jesus] said to him, "Truly, I say to you, today you will be with me in Paradise."
   Phil. 1:21. For me to live is Christ, and to die is gain.
b. 1 Cor. 15:20, 42-46, 54. In fact Christ has been raised from the dead, the first fruits of those who have fallen asleep. . . . So is it with the resurrec-tion of the dead. What is sown is perishable, what is raised is imperishable. It is sown in dishonor, it is raised in glory. It is sown in weakness, it is raised in power. It is sown a physical body, it is raised a spiritual body. If there is a physical body, there is also a spiritual body. Thus it is written, "The first man Adam became a living being"; the last Adam became a life-giving spirit. But it is not the spiri-tual which is first but the physical, and then the spiritual. . . . When the perishable puts on the im-perishable, and the mortal puts on immortality, then shall come to pass the saying that is written: "Death is swallowed up in victory."
   Job 19:25. "I know that my Redeemer lives, and at last he will stand upon the earth."
   1 John 3:2. Beloved, we are God's children now; it does not yet appear what we shall be, but we know that when he appears we shall be like him, for we shall see him as he is.
   Phil. 3:21. [The Lord Jesus Christ] will change our lowly body to be like his glorious body, by the

power which enables him even to subject all things to himself.

❡ QUESTION 58. *What comfort does the article concerning "the life everlasting" give you?*

That, since I now feel in my heart the beginning of eternal joy,[a] I shall possess, after this life, perfect blessedness, which no eye has seen, nor ear heard, nor the heart of man conceived,[b] and thereby praise God forever.[c]

a. Rom. 14:17. The kingdom of God does not mean food and drink but righteousness and peace and joy in the Holy Spirit.
b. 1 Cor. 2:9. As it is written, "What no eye has seen, nor ear heard, nor the heart of man conceived, what God has prepared for those who love him," God has revealed to us through the Spirit.
c. John 17:3. "This is eternal life, that they know thee the only true God, and Jesus Christ whom thou hast sent."

9 / TRUE FAITH

¶ QUESTION 59. *But how does it help you now that you believe all this?*

That I am righteous in Christ before God, and an heir of eternal life.[a]

a. Rom. 1:17. [In the gospel] the righteousness of God is revealed through faith for faith; as it is written, "He who through faith is righteous shall live."
Cf. Hab. 2:4.
Rom. 5:1. Since we are justified by faith, we have peace with God through our Lord Jesus Christ.
John 3:36. He who believes in the Son has eternal life.

¶ QUESTION 60. *How are you righteous before God?*

Only by true faith in Jesus Christ.[a] In spite of the fact that my conscience accuses me that I have grievously sinned against all the commandments of God, and have not kept any one of them,[b] and that I am still ever prone to all that is evil,[c] nevertheless, God, without any merit of my own,[d] out of pure grace,[e] grants me the benefits of the perfect expiation of Christ,[f] imputing to me his righteousness and holiness[g] as if I had never committed a single sin or had ever been sinful, having fulfilled myself all the obedience which Christ has carried out for me,[h] if only I accept such favor with a trusting heart.[i]

a. Rom. 3:21-22. The righteousness of God has been manifested . . . through faith in Jesus Christ for all who believe.
Cf. Phil. 3:8-11.

b. Rom. 3:9-10. What then? Are we Jews any better off? No, not at all; for I have already charged that all men, both Jews and Greeks, are under the power of sin, as it is written: "None is righteous, no, not one."

c. Rom. 7:23. I see in my members another law at war with the law of my mind and making me captive to the law of sin which dwells in my members.

d. Titus 3:5. He saved us, not because of deeds done by us in righteousness, but in virtue of his own mercy.

e. Eph. 2:8. By grace you have been saved through faith; and this is not your own doing, it is the gift of God.
Cf. Rom. 3:24.

f. 1 John 2:1-2. We have an advocate with the Father, Jesus Christ the righteous, and he is the expiation of our sins.

g. Rom. 4:3-5. Abraham believed God, and it was reckoned to him as righteousness. Now to one who works, his wages are not reckoned as a gift but as his due. And to one who does not work but trusts him who justifies the ungodly, his faith is reckoned as righteousness.

h. Rom. 4:24. It will be reckoned to us who believe

in him that raised from the dead Jesus our Lord.
Cf. 2 Cor. 5:21.

i. Rom. 3:24-25. [We] are justified by [God's] grace
as a gift, through the redemption which is in
Christ Jesus, whom God put forward as an expiation by his blood, to be received by faith. This was
to show God's righteousness, because in his divine
forbearance he had passed over former sins.

❡ QUESTION 61.   *Why do you say that you are*
righteous by faith alone?

Not because I please God by virtue of the worthi-
ness of my faith, but because the satisfaction, righteousness, and holiness of Christ alone are my righteousness before God,[a] and because I can accept it
and make it mine in no other way than by faith
alone.

a. 1 Cor. 1:30; 2:2. He is the source of your life in
Christ Jesus, whom God made our wisdom, our
righteousness and sanctification and redemption.
. . . I decided to know nothing among you except
Jesus Christ and him crucified.

LORD'S DAY 24

❡ QUESTION 62.   *But why cannot our good works*
be our righteousness before God,
or at least a part of it?

Because the righteousness which can stand before
the judgment of God must be absolutely perfect

63

and wholly in conformity with the divine Law.[a]
But even our best works in this life are all imperfect and defiled with sin.[b]

a. Gal. 3:10. All who rely on works of the law are under a curse; for it is written, "Cursed be everyone who does not abide by all things written in the book of the law, and do them."
Cf. Deut. 27:26.
b. Isa. 64:6. We have all become like one who is unclean, and all our righteous deeds are like a polluted garment. We all fade like a leaf, and our iniquities, like the wind, take us away.

❧ QUESTION 63.   *Will our good works merit nothing, even when it is God's purpose to reward them in this life, and in the future life as well?*

This reward is not given because of merit, but out of grace.[a]

a. Luke 17:10. When you have done all that is commanded you, say, "We are unworthy servants; we have only done what was our duty."

❧ QUESTION 64.   *But does not this teaching make people careless and sinful?*

No, for it is impossible for those who are ingrafted into Christ by true faith not to bring forth the fruit of gratitude.[a]

a. Matt. 7:16-17. You will know them by their fruits. Are grapes gathered from thorns, or figs from thistles? So, every sound tree bears good fruit, but the bad tree bears evil fruit.

John 15:5. "I am the vine, you are the branches. He who abides in me, and I in him, he it is that bears much fruit, for apart from me you can do nothing."

10 / THE HOLY SACRAMENTS

LORD'S DAY 25

❧ QUESTION 65. *Since, then, faith alone makes us share in Christ and all his benefits, where does such faith originate?*

The Holy Spirit creates it in our hearts[a] by the preaching of the holy gospel,[b] and confirms it by the use of the holy Sacraments.

a. Eph. 2:8. By grace you have been saved through faith; and this is not your own doing, it is the gift of God.
Cf. John 3:5.

b. 1 Peter 1:23, 25. You have been born anew, not of perishable seed but of imperishable, through the living and abiding word of God. . . . That word is the good news which was preached to you.
Cf. Matt. 28:19-20.

❧ QUESTION 66. *What are the Sacraments?*

They are visible, holy signs and seals[a] instituted by God in order that by their use he may the more fully disclose and seal to us the promise of the gospel, namely, that because of the one sacrifice of Christ accomplished on the cross he graciously grants us the forgiveness of sins and eternal life.[b]

a. Rom. 4:11. Abraham received circumcision as a sign or seal of the righteousness which he had by faith while he was still uncircumcised. The purpose was to make him the father of all who . . . thus have righteousness reckoned to them.
    Cf. Gen. 17:11; Deut. 30:6.
b. Acts 2:38; 22:16. Peter said to them, "Repent, and be baptized every one of you in the name of Jesus Christ for the forgiveness of your sins; and you shall receive the gift of the Holy Spirit. . . . Now why do you wait? Rise and be baptized, and wash away your sins, calling on his name."
    Matt. 26:28. "This is my blood of the covenant, which is poured out for many for the forgiveness of sins."
    Cf. Heb. 9.

◖ QUESTION 67. *Are both the Word and the Sacraments designed to direct our faith to the one sacrifice of Jesus Christ on the cross as the only ground of our salvation?*

Yes, indeed, for the Holy Spirit teaches in the gospel and confirms by the holy Sacraments that our whole salvation is rooted in the one sacrifice of Christ offered for us on the cross.[a]

a. Rom. 6:3. Do you not know that all of us who have been baptized into Christ Jesus were baptized into his death?

Gal. 3:27. As many of you as were baptized into Christ have put on Christ.

1 Cor. 11:26. As often as you eat this bread and drink the cup, you proclaim the Lord's death until he comes.

◖ QUESTION 68. *How many Sacraments has Christ instituted in the New Testament?*

Two, holy Baptism and the holy Supper.

11 / HOLY BAPTISM

❡ QUESTION 69. *How does holy Baptism remind and assure you that the one sacrifice of Christ on the cross avails for you?*

In this way: Christ has instituted this external washing with water[a] and by it has promised[b] that I am as certainly washed with his blood and Spirit from the uncleanness of my soul and from all my sins, as I am washed externally with water which is used to remove the dirt from my body.[c]

a. Matt. 28:19. "Go therefore and make disciples of all nations, baptizing them in the name of the Father and of the Son and of the Holy Spirit."
   Cf. Acts 2:38.
b. Matt. 3:11. "I baptize you with water for repentance, but he who is coming after me is mightier than I, whose sandals I am not worthy to carry; he will baptize you with the Holy Spirit and with fire."
   Cf. Rom. 6:3-10.
c. 1 Peter 3:21. Baptism, which corresponds to this, now saves you, not as a removal of dirt from the body but as an appeal to God for a clear conscience, through the resurrection of Jesus Christ.

❦ QUESTION 70. *What does it mean to be washed with the blood and Spirit of Christ?*

It means to have the forgiveness of sins from God, through grace, for the sake of Christ's blood·which he shed for us in his sacrifice on the cross,[a] and also to be renewed by the Holy Spirit and sanctified as members of Christ, so that we may more and more die unto sin and live in a consecrated and blameless way.[b]

a. Eph. 1:7. In [Jesus Christ] we have redemption through his blood, the forgiveness of our trespasses, according to the riches of his grace.
   Cf. Heb. 12:24; 1 Peter 1:2; Rev. 1:5-6.
b. 1 Cor. 6:11. You were washed, you were sanctified, you were justified in the name of the Lord Jesus Christ and in the Spirit of our God.
   Rom. 6:4. We were buried therefore with him by baptism into death, so that as Christ was raised from the dead by the glory of the Father, we too might walk in newness of life.
   Cf. John 1:33; Col. 2:12.

❦ QUESTION 71. *Where has Christ promised that we are as certainly washed with his blood and Spirit as with the water of baptism?*

In the institution of Baptism which runs thus: "Go THEREFORE AND MAKE DISCIPLES OF ALL NATIONS,

BAPTIZING THEM IN THE NAME OF THE FATHER AND OF THE SON AND OF THE HOLY SPIRIT."[a] "HE WHO BELIEVES AND IS BAPTIZED WILL BE SAVED: BUT HE WHO DOES NOT BELIEVE WILL BE CONDEMNED."[b] This promise is also repeated where the Scriptures call baptism "the water of rebirth"[c] and the washing away of sins.[d]

a. Matt. 28:19.
b. Mark 16:16.
c. Titus 3:5. [God] saved us through the water of rebirth and the renewing power of the Holy Spirit (N.E.B.).
d. Acts 22:16. "Rise and be baptized, and wash away your sins."

LORD'S DAY 27

❦ QUESTION 72.   *Does merely the outward washing with water itself wash away sins?*

No;[a] for only the blood of Jesus Christ and the Holy Spirit cleanse us from all sins.[b]

a. Matt. 3:11. "I baptize you with water for repentance, but he who is coming after me is mightier than I, whose sandals I am not worthy to carry; he will baptize you with the Holy Spirit and with fire." Eph. 5:25b-26. Christ loved the church and gave himself up for her, that he might sanctify her, having cleansed her by the washing of water with the word.
Cf. 1 Peter 3:21.

b. 1 John 1:7. If we walk in the light, as he is in the
    light, we have fellowship with one another, and
    the blood of Jesus his Son cleanses us from all sin.
    1 Cor. 6:11. You were washed, you were sanctified,
    you were justified in the name of the Lord Jesus
    Christ and in the Spirit of our God.

❡ QUESTION 73.   *Then why does the Holy Spirit
                  call baptism the water of rebirth
                  and the washing away of sins?*

God does not speak in this way except for a strong
reason. Not only does he teach us by Baptism that
just as the dirt of the body is taken away by water,
so our sins are removed by the blood and Spirit of
Christ;[a] but more important still, by the divine
pledge and sign he wishes to assure us that we are
just as truly washed from our sins spiritually as our
bodies are washed with water.[b]

a. Rev. 7:14. And [one of the elders] said to me,
    "These are they who have come out of the great
    tribulation; they have washed their robes and
    made them white in the blood of the Lamb."
    Cf. 1 Cor. 6:11.
b. Gal. 3:27. As many of you as were baptized into
    Christ have put on Christ.

❡ QUESTION 74.   *Are infants also to be baptized?*

Yes, because they, as well as their parents, are included in the covenant and belong to the people of

71

God.[a] Since both redemption from sin through the blood of Christ and the gift of faith from the Holy Spirit are promised to these children no less than to their parents,[b] infants are also by baptism, as a sign of the covenant, to be incorporated into the Christian church and distinguished from the children of unbelievers.[c] This was done in the Old Covenant by circumcision.[d] In the New Covenant baptism has been instituted to take its place.[e]

a. Gen. 17:7. I will establish my covenant between me and you and your descendants after you throughout their generations for an everlasting covenant, to be God to you and to your descendants after you.

   Matt. 19:14. Jesus said, "Let the children come to me, and do not hinder them; for to such belongs the kingdom of heaven."

b. Acts 2:38-39. "Repent and be baptized every one of you in the name of Jesus Christ for the forgiveness of your sins; and you shall receive the gift of the Holy Spirit."

   Cf. Isa. 44:1-3; Luke 1:15.

c. Acts 10:47. "Can anyone forbid water for baptizing these people who have received the Holy Spirit just as we have?"

   1 Cor. 7:14. The unbelieving husband is consecrated through his wife, and the unbelieving wife is consecrated through her husband. Otherwise, your children would be unclean, but as it is they are holy.

d. Cf. Gen. 17:9-14.

e. Col. 2:11-13. In him also you were circumcised
with a circumcision made without hands, by putting off the body of flesh in the circumcision of
Christ; and you were buried with him in baptism,
in which you were also raised with him through
faith in the working of God, who raised him from
the dead. And you, who were dead in trespasses
and the uncircumcision of your flesh, God made
alive together with him, having forgiven us all our
trespasses.

12 / THE LORD'S SUPPER—
HOLY COMMUNION

LORD'S DAY 28

❦ QUESTION 75.   *How are you reminded and as-*
sured in the holy Supper that
you participate in the one sacri-
fice of Christ on the cross and in
all his benefits?

In this way: Christ has commanded me and all believers to eat of this broken bread, and to drink of
this cup in remembrance of him. He has thereby
promised[a] that his body was offered and broken on
the cross for me, and his blood was shed for me, as
surely as I see with my eyes that the bread of the
Lord is broken for me, and that the cup is shared

a. See Question 77 below.

with me. Also, he has promised that he himself as certainly feeds and nourishes my soul to everlasting life with his crucified body and shed blood as I receive from the hand of the minister and actually taste the bread and the cup of the Lord which are given to me as sure signs of the body and blood of Christ.

❰ QUESTION 76. *What does it mean to eat the crucified body of Christ and to drink his shed blood?*

It is not only to embrace with a trusting heart the whole passion and death of Christ, and by it to receive the forgiveness of sins and eternal life.[a] In addition, it is to be so united more and more to his blessed body by the Holy Spirit dwelling both in Christ and in us[b] that, although he is in heaven[c] and we are on earth, we are nevertheless flesh of his flesh and bone of his bone,[d] always living and being governed by one Spirit, as the members of our bodies are governed by one soul.[e]

a. John 6:35, 40. Jesus said to them, "I am the bread of life; he who comes to me shall not hunger, and he who believes in me shall never thirst. . . . This is the will of my Father, that everyone who sees the Son and believes in him should have eternal life."
John 6:53-54. Jesus said to them, "Truly, truly, I say to you, unless you eat the flesh of the Son of

74

man and drink his blood, you have no life in you;
he who eats my flesh and drinks my blood has eternal life, and I will raise him up at the last day."

b. John 6:56. "He who eats my flesh and drinks my
blood abides in me and I in him."

c. Acts 3:20-21. May [the Lord] send the Christ appointed for you, Jesus, whom heaven must receive
until the time for establishing all that God spoke
by the mouth of his holy prophets from of old.
Cf. Acts 1:9-11; 1 Cor. 11:26.

d. Eph. 5:30. We are members of his body.
Cf. 1 Cor. 6:15, 17, 19.

e. 1 John 3:24b. By this we know that he abides in
us, by the Spirit which he has given us.
Eph. 4:15-16. We are to grow up in every way into
him who is the head, into Christ, from whom the
whole body, joined and knit together by every joint
with which it is supplied, when each part is working properly, makes bodily growth and upbuilds
itself in love.
Cf. John 6:56-58; 15:1-6.

❡ QUESTION 77. *Where has Christ promised that
he will feed and nourish believ-
ers with his body and blood just
as surely as they eat of this
broken bread and drink of this
cup?*

In the institution of the holy Supper which reads:
THE LORD JESUS ON THE NIGHT WHEN HE WAS BE-

75

TRAYED TOOK BREAD, AND WHEN HE HAD GIVEN
THANKS, HE BROKE IT, AND SAID, "THIS IS MY BODY
WHICH IS FOR YOU. DO THIS IN REMEMBRANCE OF
ME." IN THE SAME WAY ALSO THE CUP, AFTER SUP-
PER, SAYING, "THIS CUP IS THE NEW COVENANT IN MY
BLOOD. DO THIS, AS OFTEN AS YOU DRINK IT, IN RE-
MEMBRANCE OF ME." FOR AS OFTEN AS YOU EAT THIS
BREAD AND DRINK THE CUP, YOU PROCLAIM THE
LORD'S DEATH UNTIL HE COMES.[a]

This promise is also repeated by the apostle Paul:
WHEN WE BLESS "THE CUP OF BLESSING," IS IT NOT A
MEANS OF SHARING IN THE BLOOD OF CHRIST? WHEN
WE BREAK THE BREAD, IS IT NOT A MEANS OF SHAR-
ING THE BODY OF CHRIST? BECAUSE THERE IS ONE
LOAF, WE, MANY AS WE ARE, ARE ONE BODY; FOR IT
IS ONE LOAF OF WHICH WE ALL PARTAKE.[b]

a. 1 Cor. 11:23-26.
    Cf. Matt. 26:26-28; Mark 14:22-24; Luke 22:19.
b. 1 Cor. 10:16-17 (N.E.B.).

❡ QUESTION 78.   *Do the bread and wine become
the very body and blood of
Christ?*

No, for as the water in baptism is not changed into
the blood of Christ, nor becomes the washing away
of sins by itself, but is only a divine sign and con-
firmation of it, so also in the Lord's Supper[a] the
sacred bread does not become the body of Christ

itself,[b] although, in accordance with the nature and usage of sacraments,[c] it is called the body of Christ.

a. Matt. 26:26-29. As they were eating, Jesus took bread, and blessed, and broke it, and gave it to the disciples and said, "Take, eat; this is my body." And he took a cup, and when he had given thanks he gave it to them, saying, "Drink of it, all of you; for this is my blood of the covenant, which is poured out for many for the forgiveness of sins. I tell you I shall not drink again of this fruit of the vine until that day when I drink it new with you in my Father's kingdom."

b. 1 Cor. 11:26-28. As often as you eat this bread and drink the cup, you proclaim the Lord's death until he comes. Whoever, therefore, eats the bread or drinks the cup of the Lord in an unworthy manner will be guilty of profaning the body and blood of the Lord. Let a man examine himself, and so eat of the bread and drink of the cup.

c. 1 Cor. 10:1-4. I want you to know, brethren, that our fathers were all under the cloud, and all passed through the sea, and all were baptized into Moses in the cloud and in the sea, and all ate the same spiritual food and all drank the same spiritual drink. For they drank from the spiritual Rock which followed them, and the Rock was Christ.
Cf. Gen. 17:10-19; Exod. 12:27, 43, 48.

❡ QUESTION 79. *Then why does Christ call the bread his body, and the cup his blood, or the New Covenant in his blood, and why does the apostle Paul call the Supper "a means of sharing" in the body and blood of Christ?*

Christ does not speak in this way except for a strong reason. He wishes to teach us by it that as bread and wine sustain this temporal life so his crucified body and shed blood are the true food and drink of our souls for eternal life.[a] Even more, he wishes to assure us by this visible sign and pledge that we come to share in his true body and blood through the working of the Holy Spirit as surely as we receive with our mouth these holy tokens in remembrance of him,[b] and that all his sufferings and his death are our own as certainly as if we had ourselves suffered and rendered satisfaction in our own persons.

a. John 6:51, 55. I am the living bread which came down from heaven; if anyone eats of this bread, he will live forever; and the bread which I shall give for the life of the world is my flesh. . . . For my flesh is food indeed, and my blood is drink indeed.

b. 1 Cor. 10:16-17. When we bless "the cup of blessing," is it not a means of sharing in the blood of Christ? When we break the bread, is it not a means of sharing in the body of Christ? Because there is one loaf, we, many as we are, are one body; for it is one loaf of which we all partake (N.E.B.).

℄ QUESTION 80. *What difference is there between the Lord's Supper and the papal Mass?*

The Lord's Supper testifies to us that we have complete forgiveness of all our sins through the one sacrifice of Jesus Christ which he himself has accomplished on the cross once for all;[a] (and that through the Holy Spirit we are incorporated into Christ,[b] who is now in heaven with his true body at the right hand of the Father[c] and is there to be worshiped.[d]) But the Mass teaches that the living and the dead do not have forgiveness of sins through the sufferings of Christ unless Christ is again offered for them daily by the priest (and that Christ is bodily under the form of bread and wine and is therefore to be worshiped in them). Therefore the Mass is fundamentally a complete denial of the once for all sacrifice and passion of Jesus Christ[e] (and as such an idolatry to be condemned).

NOTE: This question first appeared in part in the second edition. The sections in parentheses were added in the third.

a. Heb. 7:27; 9:12, 25-28. He has no need, like those

79

high priests, to offer sacrifices daily, first for his own sins and then for those of the people; he did this once for all when he offered up himself. . . . He entered once for all into the Holy Place, taking not the blood of goats and calves but his own blood, thus securing an eternal redemption. . . . Nor was it to offer himself repeatedly, as the high priest enters the Holy Place yearly with blood not his own; for then he would have had to suffer repeatedly since the foundation of the world. But as it is, he has appeared once for all at the end of the age to put away sin by the sacrifice of himself. And just as it is appointed for men to die once, and after that comes judgment, so Christ, having been offered once to bear the sins of many, will appear a second time, not to deal with sin but to save those who are eagerly waiting for him.

Cf. Heb. 10:10-18.

b. 1 Cor. 6:17. He who is united to the Lord becomes one spirit with him.

c. Heb. 1:3; 8:1. When he had made purification for sins, he sat down at the right hand of the Majesty on high. . . . The point in what we are saying is this: we have such a high priest, one who is seated at the right hand of the throne of the Majesty in heaven.

d. John 20:17. I have not yet ascended to the Father; but go to my brethren and say to them, I am ascending to my Father and your Father, to my God and your God.

Acts 7:55-56. He, full of the Holy Spirit, gazed into heaven and saw the glory of God, and Jesus standing at the right hand of God; and he said, "Behold, I see the heavens opened, and the Son of man standing at the right hand of God."

Col. 3:1. If then you have been raised with Christ, seek the things that are above, where Christ is, seated at the right hand of God.

Cf. John 4:21-24; Phil. 3:20; 1 Thess. 1:10.

e. Heb. 9:25-26; 10:11-14. Nor was it to offer himself repeatedly, as the high priest enters the Holy Place yearly with blood not his own; for then he would have had to suffer repeatedly since the foundation of the world. But as it is, he has appeared once for all at the end of the age to put away sin by the sacrifice of himself. . . . Every priest stands daily at his service, offering repeatedly the same sacrifices, which can never take away sins. But when Christ had offered for all time a single sacrifice for sins, he sat down at the right hand of God, then to wait until his enemies should be made a stool for his feet. For by a single offering he has perfected for all time those who are sanctified.

13 / CHURCH DISCIPLINE

❡ QUESTION 81.   *Who ought to come to the table of the Lord?*

Those who are displeased with themselves for their sins,[a] and who nevertheless trust that these sins have been forgiven them and that their remaining weakness is covered by the passion and death of Christ,[b] and who also desire more and more to strengthen their faith and improve their life.[c] The impenitent and hypocrites, however, eat and drink judgment to themselves.[d]

a. Matt. 5:3. "Blessed are the poor in spirit, for theirs is the kingdom of heaven."
b. Ps. 103:2-3. Bless the Lord, O my soul, and forget not all his benefits, who forgives all your iniquity, who heals all your diseases.
   Eph. 1:7. In [Jesus Christ] we have redemption through his blood, the forgiveness of our trespasses, according to the riches of his grace.
c. Matt. 5:5. "Blessed are the meek, for they shall inherit the earth."
   Ps. 116:12-14. What shall I render to the Lord for all his bounty to me? I will lift up the cup of salvation and call on the name of the Lord, I will pay my vows to the Lord in the presence of all his people.
d. 1 Cor. 10:21; 11:28. You cannot drink the cup of the Lord and the cup of demons. You cannot partake of the table of the Lord and the table of demons. . . . Let a man examine himself, and so eat of the bread and drink of the cup.

❦ QUESTION 82. *Should those who show them-*
selves to be unbelievers and ene-
mies of God by their confession
and life be admitted to this Sup-
per?

No, for then the covenant of God would be pro-
faned and his wrath provoked against the whole
congregation.[a] According to the ordinance of Christ
and his apostles, therefore, the Christian church is
under obligation, by the office of the keys, to ex-
clude such persons until they amend their lives.

a. 1 Cor. 11:20, 26-29, 34. When you meet together, it
is not the Lord's Supper that you eat. . . . For as
often as you eat this bread and drink the cup, you
proclaim the Lord's death until he comes. Whoever, therefore, eats the bread or drinks the cup of
the Lord in an unworthy manner will be guilty of
profaning the body and blood of the Lord. Let a
man examine himself, and so eat of the bread and
drink of the cup. For anyone who eats and drinks
without discerning the body eats and drinks judgment upon himself. . . . If anyone is hungry, let
him eat at home—lest you come together to be condemned.
Cf. Isa. 1:11-15; 66:3; Ps. 50:16.

LORD'S DAY 31

❦ QUESTION 83. *What is the office of the keys?*

The preaching of the holy gospel and Christian discipline. By these two means the kingdom of heaven is opened to believers and shut against unbelievers.[a]

a. Matt. 16:19. "I will give you the keys of the kingdom of heaven, and whatever you bind on earth shall be bound in heaven, and whatever you loose on earth shall be loosed in heaven."

John 20:23. "If you forgive the sins of any, they are forgiven; if you retain the sins of any, they are retained."

❡ QUESTION 84. *How is the kingdom of heaven opened and shut by the preaching of the holy gospel?*

In this way: The kingdom of heaven is opened when it is proclaimed and openly testified to believers, one and all, according to the command of Christ, that as often as they accept the promise of the gospel with true faith all their sins are truly forgiven them by God for the sake of Christ's gracious work. On the contrary, the wrath of God and eternal condemnation fall upon all unbelievers and hypocrites as long as they do not repent.[a] It is according to this witness of the gospel that God will judge the one and the other in this life and in the life to come.

a. Matt. 28:19. "Go therefore and make disciples of all nations, baptizing them in the name of the Father and of the Son and of the Holy Spirit."

John 20:21-23. Jesus said to them again, "Peace be with you. As the Father has sent me, even so I send you." And when he had said this, he breathed on them, and said to them, "Receive the Holy Spirit. If you forgive the sins of any, they are forgiven; if you retain the sins of any, they are retained."

Matt. 16:19. "I will give you the keys of the kingdom of heaven, and whatever you bind on earth shall be bound in heaven, and whatever you loose on earth shall be loosed in heaven."

Cf. John 3:18-36; Rom. 2:2-17.

❡ QUESTION 85. *How is the kingdom of heaven shut and opened by Christian discipline?*

In this way: Christ commanded that those who bear the Christian name in an unchristian way either in doctrine or in life should be given brotherly admonition. If they do not give up their errors or evil ways, notification is given to the church or to those ordained for this by the church. Then, if they do not change after this warning, they are forbidden to partake of the holy Sacraments and are thus excluded from the communion of the church and by God himself from the kingdom of Christ.[a] However, if they promise and show real amendment, they are received again as members of Christ and of the church.[b]

a. Matt. 18:15-18. "If your brother sins against you,

go and tell him his fault, between you and him alone. If he listens to you, you have gained your brother. But if he does not listen, take one or two others along with you, that every word may be confirmed by the evidence of two or three witnesses. If he refuses to listen to them, tell it to the church; and if he refuses to listen even to the church, let him be to you as a Gentile and a tax collector. Truly, I say to you, whatever you bind on earth shall be bound in heaven, and whatever you loose on earth shall be loosed in heaven."

1 Cor. 5:11-13. I wrote to you not to associate with anyone who bears the name of brother if he is guilty of immorality or greed, or is an idolator, reviler, drunkard, or robber—not even to eat with such a one. For what have I to do with judging outsiders? Is it not those inside the church whom you are to judge? God judges those outside. Drive out the wicked person from among you.

Cf. 2 Thess. 3:14; 2 John 10-11.

b. Luke 15:18. "I will arise and go to my father, and I will say to him, 'Father, I have sinned against heaven and before you.'"

Cf. 2 Cor. 2:6-11.

PART III

*Man's Gratitude and Obedience—New Life
Through the Holy Spirit*

---

14 / DISCIPLESHIP AND GOOD WORKS

LORD'S DAY 32

❮ QUESTION 86. *Since we are redeemed from our
sin and its wretched consequen-
ces by grace through Christ without any merit of our own, why
must we do good works?*

Because just as Christ has redeemed us with his
blood he also renews us through his Holy Spirit according to his own image, so that with our whole
life we may show ourselves grateful to God for his
goodness[a] and that he may be glorified through us;[b]
and further, so that we ourselves may be assured of
our faith by its fruits[c] and by our reverent behavior
may win our neighbors to Christ.[d]

a. Rom. 6:13; 12:1. Do not yield your members to sin
   as instruments of wickedness, but yield yourselves
   to God as men who have been brought from death
   to life, and your members to God as instruments

of righteousness. . . . I appeal to you therefore, brethren, by the mercies of God, to present your bodies as a living sacrifice, holy and acceptable to God, which is your spiritual worship.

Cf. 1 Peter 2:5-10.

b. Matt. 5:16. Let your light so shine before men, that they may see your good works and give glory to your Father who is in heaven.

1 Cor. 6:19-20. Do you not know that your body is a temple of the Holy Spirit within you, which you have from God? You are not your own; you were bought with a price. So glorify God in your body.

Cf. 1 Peter 2:12.

c. Matt. 7:17. Every sound tree bears good fruit, but the bad tree bears evil fruit.

Cf. Luke 13:6-9.

Gal. 5:22-24. The fruit of the Spirit is love, joy, peace, patience, kindness, goodness, faithfulness, gentleness, self-control; against such there is no law. And those who belong to Christ Jesus have crucified the flesh with its passions and desires.

d. 1 Peter 3:1-2. You women must accept the authority of your husbands, so that if there are any of them who disbelieve the gospel they may be won over, without a word being said, by observing the chaste and reverent behavior of their wives (N.E.B.).

❡ QUESTION 87. *Can those who do not turn to God from their ungrateful, impenitent life be saved?*

Certainly not! Scripture says, "Surely you know

that the unjust will never come into possession of the kingdom of God. Make no mistake: no fornicator or idolater, none who are guilty either of adultery or of homosexual perversion, no thieves or grabbers or drunkards or slanderers or swindlers, will possess the kingdom of God."[a]

a. 1 Cor. 6:9-10 (N.E.B.).
   Cf. Gal. 5:19-21; Eph. 5:5-33; 1 John 3:14-24.

¶ QUESTION 88. *How many parts are there to the true repentance or conversion of man?*

Two: the dying of the old self and the birth of the new.[a]

a. Rom. 6:4-6. We were buried therefore with him by baptism into death, so that as Christ was raised from the dead by the glory of the Father, we too might walk in newness of life. For if we have been united with him in a death like his, we shall certainly be united with him in a resurrection like his. We know that our old self was crucified with him so that the sinful body might be destroyed, and we might no longer be enslaved to sin.
   2 Cor. 5:17. Therefore, if anyone is in Christ, he is a new creation, the old has passed away, behold the new has come.
   Cf. Eph. 4:22-24; Col. 3:5-10; 1 Cor. 5:7.

❡ QUESTION 89. *What is the dying of the old self?*

Sincere sorrow over our sins and more and more to hate them and to flee from them.ᵃ

a. Rom. 8:13. If you live according to the flesh you will die, but if by the Spirit you put to death the deeds of the body you will live.
2 Cor. 7:10. Godly grief produces a repentance that leads to salvation and brings no regret, but worldly grief produces death.
Cf. Joel 2:13; Ps. 51:3, 8, 17.

❡ QUESTION 90. *What is the birth of the new self?*

Complete joy in God through Christᵃ and a strong desire to live according to the will of God in all good works.ᵇ

a. Rom. 5:1. Since we are justified by faith, we have peace with God through our Lord Jesus Christ.
Cf. Rom. 14:17; Isa. 57:15.
b. Gal. 2:20. I have been crucified with Christ; it is no longer I who live, but Christ who lives in me; and the life I now live in the flesh I live by faith in the Son of God, who loved me and gave himself for me.
Cf. Rom. 6:10-11.

❡ QUESTION 91. *But what are good works?*

Only those which are done out of true faith,ᵃ in

accordance with the Law of God,[b] and for his glory,[c] and not those based on our own opinion or on the traditions of men.[d]

a. Rom. 14:20b, 22b-23. Everything is indeed clean, but it is wrong for anyone to make others fall by what he eats . . . happy is he who has no reason to judge himself for what he approves. But he who has doubts is condemned, if he eats, because he does not act from faith; for whatever does not proceed from faith is sin.

b. 1 Sam. 15:22. Samuel said, "Has the Lord as great delight in burnt offerings and sacrifices, as in obeying the voice of the Lord? Behold, to obey is better than sacrifice, and to hearken than the fat of rams."
Cf. Eph. 2:10.

c. 1 Cor. 10:31. Whether you eat or drink, or whatever you do, do all to the glory of God.

d. Deut. 12:32. "Everything that I command you you shall be careful to do; you shall not add to it or take from it."
Matt. 15:9. "In vain do they worship me, teaching as doctrines the precepts of men."
Cf. Isa. 29:13; Ezek. 20:18-19.

LORD'S DAY 34

❦ QUESTION 92. *What is the Law of God?*

God spoke all these words saying:

First Commandment

"I AM THE LORD YOUR GOD, WHO BROUGHT YOU OUT

OF THE LAND OF EGYPT, OUT OF THE HOUSE OF BOND-
AGE. YOU SHALL HAVE NO OTHER GODS BEFORE ME."

Second Commandment

"YOU SHALL NOT MAKE YOURSELF A GRAVEN IMAGE,
OR ANY LIKENESS OF ANYTHING THAT IS IN HEAVEN
ABOVE, OR THAT IS IN THE EARTH BENEATH, OR THAT
IS IN THE WATER UNDER THE EARTH; YOU SHALL NOT
BOW DOWN TO THEM OR SERVE THEM; FOR I THE
LORD YOUR GOD AM A JEALOUS GOD, VISITING THE
INIQUITY OF THE FATHERS UPON THE CHILDREN TO
THE THIRD AND THE FOURTH GENERATION OF THOSE
WHO HATE ME, BUT SHOWING STEADFAST LOVE TO
THOUSANDS OF THOSE WHO LOVE ME AND KEEP MY
COMMANDMENTS."

Third Commandment

"YOU SHALL NOT TAKE THE NAME OF THE LORD YOUR
GOD IN VAIN; FOR THE LORD WILL NOT HOLD HIM
GUILTLESS WHO TAKES HIS NAME IN VAIN."

Fourth Commandment

"REMEMBER THE SABBATH DAY, TO KEEP IT HOLY.
SIX DAYS YOU SHALL LABOR, AND DO ALL YOUR WORK;
BUT THE SEVENTH DAY IS A SABBATH TO THE LORD
YOUR GOD; IN IT YOU SHALL NOT DO ANY WORK, YOU,
OR YOUR SON, OR YOUR DAUGHTER, YOUR MANSER-
VANT, OR YOUR MAIDSERVANT, OR YOUR CATTLE, OR
THE SOJOURNER WHO IS WITHIN YOUR GATES; FOR IN
SIX DAYS THE LORD MADE HEAVEN AND EARTH, THE
SEA, AND ALL THAT IS IN THEM, AND RESTED THE SEV-

ENTH DAY; THEREFORE THE LORD BLESSED THE SAB-
BATH DAY AND HALLOWED IT."

Fifth Commandment

"HONOR YOUR FATHER AND YOUR MOTHER, THAT
YOUR DAYS MAY BE LONG IN THE LAND WHICH THE
LORD YOUR GOD GIVES YOU."

Sixth Commandment

"YOU SHALL NOT KILL."

Seventh Commandment

"YOU SHALL NOT COMMIT ADULTERY."

Eighth Commandment

"YOU SHALL NOT STEAL."

Ninth Commandment

"YOU SHALL NOT BEAR FALSE WITNESS AGAINST YOUR
NEIGHBOR."

Tenth Commandment

"YOU SHALL NOT COVET YOUR NEIGHBOR'S HOUSE;
YOU SHALL NOT COVET YOUR NEIGHBOR'S WIFE, OR HIS
MANSERVANT, OR HIS MAIDSERVANT, OR HIS OX, OR
HIS ASS, OR ANYTHING THAT IS YOUR NEIGHBOR'S."[a]

a. Exod. 20:1-17.
   Cf. Deut. 5:6-21.

¶ QUESTION 93. *How are these commandments
                 divided?*

Into two tables,[a] the first of which teaches us in

93

four commandments how we ought to live in relation to God; the other, in six commandments, what we owe to our neighbor.[b]

a. Exod. 34:28-29. He was there with the Lord forty days and forty nights; he neither ate bread nor drank water. And he wrote upon the tables the words of the covenant, the ten commandments. When Moses came down from Mount Sinai, with the two tables of the testimony in his hand as he came down from the mountain, Moses did not know that the skin of his face shone because he had been talking with God.
Cf. Deut. 4:13; 10:3.

b. Matt. 22:37-39. [Jesus] said to him, "You shall love the Lord your God with all your heart, and with all your soul, and with all your mind. This is the great and first commandment. And a second is like it, You shall love your neighbor as yourself."

15 / LOVE AND HONOR TO GOD— THE FIRST TABLE OF THE LAW

❧ QUESTION 94. *What does the Lord require in the first commandment?*

That I must avoid and flee all idolatry,[a] sorcery, enchantments,[b] invocation of saints or other creatures[c] because of the risk of losing my salvation. Indeed, I ought properly to acknowledge the only true God,[d] trust in him alone,[e] in humility[f] and patience[g] expect all good from him only,[h] and love,[i] fear[j] and honor[k] him with my whole heart. In short, I should rather turn my back on all creatures than do the least thing against his will.[l]

a. 1 Cor. 10:5-14. With most of [our fathers] God was not pleased; for they were overthrown in the wilderness. Now these things are warnings to us, not to desire evil as they did. Do not be idolators as some of them were. . . . We must not indulge in immorality as some of them did. . . . We must not put the Lord to the test . . . nor grumble. . . . Now these things happened as a warning, but they are written down for our instruction. . . . Therefore, let anyone who thinks that he stands take heed lest he fall. . . . My beloved, shun the worship of idols.
Cf. 1 Cor. 6:9-10.

b. Lev. 19:31. "Do not turn to mediums or wizards; do not seek them out, to be defiled by them: I am the Lord your God."
Cf. Deut. 18:10-12.

c. Matt. 4:10. Jesus said to him, "Begone, Satan! for it is written, 'You shall worship the Lord your God and him only shall you serve.'"
Cf. Rev. 19:10; 22:8-9.

d. John 17:3. "This is eternal life, that they know thee the only true God, and Jesus Christ whom thou hast sent."

e. Jer. 17:5, 7. Thus says the Lord: "Cursed is the man who trusts in man and makes flesh his arm, whose heart turns away from the Lord. . . . Blessed is the man who trusts in the Lord, whose trust is the Lord."

f. 1 Peter 5:5-6. You that are younger be subject to the elders. Clothe yourselves, all of you, with humility toward one another, for "God opposes the proud, but gives grace to the humble."

g. Heb. 10:36. You have need of endurance, so that you may do the will of God and receive what is promised.
    Cf. Rom. 5:3-4; Phil. 2:14; Col. 1:11-12.

h. James 1:17. Every good endowment and every perfect gift is from above, coming down from the Father of lights with whom there is no variation or shadow due to change.
    Cf. Ps. 104:27-28.

i. Deut. 6:5. You shall love the Lord your God with all your heart, and with all your soul, and with all your might.
    Cf. Matt. 22:37.

j. Deut. 6:2. Fear the Lord your God, you and your son and your son's son, by keeping all his statutes and his commandments, which I command you, all the days of your life.
    Cf. Ps. 111:10; Prov. 1:7; 9:10; Matt. 10:28.

k. Rev. 5:13. I heard every creature in heaven and on earth and under the earth and in the sea, and all therein, saying, "To him who sits upon the throne and to the Lamb be blessing and honor and glory and might forever and ever!"

l. Matt. 10:37. "He who loves father or mother more than me is not worthy of me; and he who loves son

or daughter more than me is not worthy of me."
Cf. Matt. 5:29-30; Acts 5:29.

❦ QUESTION 95.   *What is idolatry?*

It is to imagine or possess something in which to
put one's trust in place of or beside the one true
God who has revealed himself in his Word.[a]

a. Gal. 4:8-9. Formerly, when you did not know God,
    you were in bondage to beings that by nature are
    no gods; but now that you have come to know God,
    or rather to be known by God, how can you turn
    back again to the weak and beggarly elemental
    spirits, whose slaves you want to be once more?
    Cf. 1 Chron. 16:26; 2 Chron. 16:12; Phil. 3:18-19;
    Eph. 2:12; 2 John 1:9.

LORD'S DAY 35

❦ QUESTION 96.   *What does God require in the
                  second commandment?*

That we should not represent[a] him or worship him
in any other manner than he has commanded in
his Word.[b]

a. Acts 17:29. Being then God's offspring, we ought
    not to think that the Deity is like gold, or silver, or
    stone, a representation by the art and imagination
    of man.
    Cf. Deut. 4:15-19; Isa. 40:18-25; Rom. 1:23.
b. 1 Sam. 15:23. "Rebellion is as the sin of divination,
    and stubbornness is as iniquity and idolatry. Be-

cause you have rejected the word of the Lord, he has also rejected you from being king."
Cf. Deut. 12:30-32; Matt. 15:9.

❡ QUESTION 97. *Should we, then, not make any images at all?*

God cannot and should not be pictured in any way. As for creatures, although they may indeed be portrayed, God forbids making or having any likeness of them in order to worship them, or to use them to serve him.[a]

a. Exod. 23:24; 34:13-14. You shall not bow down to their gods, nor serve them, nor do according to their works, but you shall utterly overthrow them and break their pillars in pieces. You shall tear down their altars and break their pillars, and cut down their Asherim (for you shall worship no other god, for the Lord, whose name is Jealous, is a jealous God).
Cf. Num. 33:52; Deut. 4:15-16; 7:5; 12:3-4; 2 Kings 18:3-4.

❡ QUESTION 98. *But may not pictures be tolerated in churches in place of books for unlearned people?*

No, for we must not try to be wiser than God who does not want his people to be taught by means of lifeless idols,[a] but through the living preaching of his Word.[b]

a. Hab. 2:18-20. What profit is an idol when its maker has shaped it, a metal image, a teacher of lies? For the workman trusts in his own creation when he makes dumb idols! Woe to him who says to a wooden thing, Awake; to a dumb stone, Arise! Can this give revelation? Behold, it is overlaid with gold and silver, and there is no breath at all in it. But the Lord is in his holy temple; let all the earth keep silence before him.

Cf. Jer. 10:8.

b. 2 Tim. 3:16-17. All scripture is inspired by God and profitable for teaching, for reproof, for correction, and for training in righteousness, that the man of God may be complete, equipped for every good work.

Cf. 2 Peter 1:19.

℃ QUESTION 99. *What is required in the third commandment?*

That we must not profane or abuse the name of God by cursing,[a] by perjury,[b] or by unnecessary oaths.[c] Nor are we to participate in such horrible sins by keeping quiet and thus giving silent consent. In a word, we must not use the holy name of God except with fear and reverence[d] so that he may be rightly confessed[e] and addressed[f] by us, and be glorified in all our words and works.[g]

a. Lev. 24:11, 13, 16. The Israelite woman's son blasphemed the Name, and cursed. And they brought him to Moses. . . . And the Lord said to Moses, . . . "He who blasphemes the name of the Lord shall be put to death; the sojourner as well as the native, when he blasphemes the Name, shall be put to death."

b. Lev. 19:12. "You shall not swear by my name falsely, and so profane the name of your God: I am the Lord."

c. Matt. 5:37. "Let what you say be simply 'Yes' or 'No'; anything more than this comes from evil." Cf. James 5:12.

d. Ps. 99:3. Let them praise thy great and terrible name! Holy is he!
Deut. 28:58. "Fear this glorious and awful name, the Lord your God."

e. Matt. 10:32. "Everyone who acknowledges me before men, I also will acknowledge before my Father who is in heaven."

f. 1 Tim. 2:8. I desire then that in every place the men should pray, lifting holy hands without anger or quarreling.

g. Col. 3:17. Whatever you do, in word or deed, do everything in the name of the Lord Jesus, giving thanks to God the Father through him.
Cf. Rom. 2:24; 1 Tim. 6:1.

¶ QUESTION 100. *Is it, therefore, so great a sin to blaspheme God's name by cursing and swearing that God is also angry with those who do not try to prevent and forbid it as much as they can?*

Yes, indeed;[a] for no sin is greater or provokes his wrath more than the profaning of his name. That is why he commanded it to be punished with death.[b]

a. Lev. 5:1. "If anyone sins in that he hears a public adjuration to testify and though he is a witness, whether he has seen or come to know the matter, yet does not speak, he shall bear his iniquity."

b. Lev. 24:15-16. "Say to the people of Israel, Whoever curses his God shall bear his sin. He who blasphemes the name of the Lord shall be put to death."

LORD'S DAY 37

¶ QUESTION 101. *But may we not swear oaths by the name of God in a devout manner?*

Yes, when the civil authorities require it of their subjects, or when it is otherwise needed to maintain and promote fidelity and truth, to the glory of God and the welfare of our neighbor. Such oath-taking is grounded in God's Word[a] and has therefore been rightly used by God's people under the Old and New Covenants.[b]

a. Deut. 6:13. You shall fear the Lord your God; you shall serve him, and swear by his name.
   Cf. Deut. 10:20; Isa. 48:1; Heb. 6:16.
b. Cf. Gen. 21:24; 31:53-54; Josh. 9:15, 19; 1 Sam. 24:22; 2 Sam. 3:35; 1 Kings 1:28-30; Rom. 1:9; 2 Cor. 1:23.

¶ QUESTION 102. *May we also swear by the saints or other creatures?*

No; for a lawful oath is a calling upon God, as the only searcher of hearts, to bear witness to the truth, and to punish me if I swear falsely.[a] No creature deserves such honor.[b]

a. 2 Cor. 1:23. I call God to witness against me—it was to spare you that I refrained from coming to Corinth.
b. Matt. 5:34-35. I say to you, Do not swear at all, either by heaven, for it is the throne of God, or by the earth, for it is his footstool, or by Jerusalem, for it is the city of the great King.

LORD'S DAY 38

¶ QUESTION 103. *What does God require in the fourth commandment?*

First, that the ministry of the gospel and Christian education be maintained,[a] and that I diligently at-

tend church, especially on the Lord's day,[b] to hear
the Word of God,[c] to participate in the holy Sacraments,[d] to call publicly upon the Lord,[e] and to give
Christian service to those in need.[f] Second, that I
cease from my evil works all the days of my life,
allow the Lord to work in me through his Spirit,
and thus begin in this life the eternal Sabbath.[g]

a. 2 Tim. 2:2; 3:15. What you have heard from me
    before many witnesses entrust to faithful men who
    will be able to teach others also. . . . From child-
    hood you have been acquainted with the sacred
    writings which are able to instruct you for salva-
    tion through faith in Christ Jesus.
    Cf. 1 Tim. 4:13-16; 5:17; 1 Cor. 9:13-14.

b. Lev. 23:3. Six days shall work be done; but on the
    seventh day is a sabbath of solemn rest, a holy con-
    vocation; you shall do no work; it is a sabbath to
    the Lord in all your dwellings.
    Acts 2:42, 46. They devoted themselves to the apos-
    tles' teaching and fellowship, to the breaking of
    bread and the prayers. . . . And day by day, attend-
    ing the temple together and breaking bread in
    their homes, they partook of food with glad and
    generous hearts.
    Cf. Ps. 68:26.

c. Rom. 10:17. Faith comes from what is heard, and
    what is heard comes by the preaching of Christ.
    1 Cor. 14:19. In church I would rather speak five
    words with my mind, in order to instruct others,
    than ten thousand words in a tongue.
    Cf. 1 Cor. 14:29, 31.

d. 1 Cor. 11:24. The Lord Jesus said, "Do this in remembrance of me."

e. 1 Tim. 2:1. First of all, then, I urge that supplica-
tions, prayers, intercessions, and thanksgivings be
made for all men.

f. 1 Cor. 16:2. On the first day of every week, each
of you is to put something aside and store it up, as
he may prosper, so that contributions need not be
made when I come.

g. Isa. 66:23. "From new moon to new moon, and
from sabbath to sabbath, all flesh shall come to
worship before me," says the Lord.

16 / LOVE AND SERVICE OF THE NEIGHBOR— THE SECOND TABLE OF THE LAW

LORD'S DAY 39

℄ QUESTION 104. *What does God require in the
fifth commandment?*

That I show honor, love, and faithfulness to my
father and mother and to all who are set in authority over me; that I submit myself with respectful
obedience to all their careful instruction and discipline;[a] and that I also bear patiently their failures,[b]
since it is God's will to govern us by their hand.[c]

a. Eph. 6:1-4. Children, obey your parents in the
Lord, for this is right. "Honor your father and
mother" (this is the first commandment with a
promise), "that it may be well with you and that

you may live long on the earth." Fathers, do not provoke your children to anger, but bring them up in the discipline and instruction of the Lord. Rom. 13:1-2. Let every person be subject to the governing authorities. For there is no authority except from God, and those that exist have been instituted by God. Therefore he who resists the authorities resists what God has appointed, and those who resist will incur judgment.

Cf. Prov. 1:8; 4; 20:20; Deut. 6:6-9.

b. Prov. 23:22. Hearken to your father who begot you, and do not despise your mother when she is old.

1 Peter 2:18. Servants, be submissive to your masters with all respect, not only to the kind and gentle but also to the overbearing.

c. Col. 3:18-21. Wives, be subject to your husbands, as is fitting in the Lord. Husbands, love your wives, and do not be harsh with them. Children, obey your parents in everything, for this pleases the Lord. Fathers, do not provoke your children, lest they become discouraged.

Cf. Eph. 6:1-9; Rom. 13:1-8; Matt. 22:21.

LORD'S DAY 40

❦ QUESTION 105. *What does God require in the sixth commandment?*

That I am not to abuse, hate, injure, or kill my neighbor, either with thought, or by word or gesture, much less by deed, whether by myself or through another,[a] but to lay aside all desire for revenge;[b] and that I do not harm myself or willfully expose myself to danger.[c] This is why the authorities are armed with the means to prevent murder.[d]

a. Matt. 5:21-22. "You have heard that it was said to the men of old, 'You shall not kill; and whoever kills shall be liable to judgment.' But I say to you that everyone who is angry with his brother shall be liable to judgment; whoever insults his brother shall be liable to the council, and whoever says, 'You fool!' shall be liable to the hell of fire."

b. Rom. 12:19. Beloved, never avenge yourselves, but leave it to the wrath of God; for it is written, "Vengeance is mine, I will repay, says the Lord."
Cf. Eph. 4:26; Matt. 5:25, 39-40; 18:35.

c. Matt. 4:7. "You shall not tempt the Lord your God."

d. Rom. 13:4. The [governing authority] is God's servant for your good. But if you do wrong, be afraid, for he does not bear the sword in vain; he is the servant of God to execute his wrath on the wrongdoer.
Cf. Gen. 9:6; Matt. 26:52.

❧ QUESTION 106. *But does this commandment speak only of killing?*

In forbidding murder God means to teach us that he abhors the root of murder, which is envy,[a] hatred,[b] anger, and desire for revenge,[c] and that he regards all these as hidden murder.[d]

a. Gal. 5:19-21. The works of the flesh are plain . . . enmity, strife, jealousy, anger, selfishness, dissension, party spirit, envy. . . . I warn you, as I warned you before, that those who do such things shall not inherit the kingdom of God.
Cf. Rom. 1:29.

b. 1 John 2:9. He who says he is in the light and hates his brother is in the darkness still.

c. Rom. 12:19. Beloved, never avenge yourselves, but leave it to the wrath of God; for it is written, "Vengeance is mine, I will repay, says the Lord."

d. 1 John 3:15. Anyone who hates his brother is a murderer, and you know that no murderer has eternal life abiding in him.

❰ QUESTION 107. *Is it enough, then, if we do not kill our neighbor in any of these ways?*

No; for when God condemns envy, hatred, and anger, he requires us to love our neighbor as ourselves,[a] to show patience, peace, gentleness,[b] mercy,[c] and friendliness[d] toward him, to prevent injury to him as much as we can,[e] also to do good to our enemies.[f]

a. Matt. 22:39. "You shall love your neighbor as yourself."
Matt. 7:12. "Whatever you wish that men would do to you, do so to them; for this is the law and the prophets."

b. Rom. 12:10. Love one another with brotherly affec-

tion; outdo one another in showing honor.
Cf. Eph. 4:2; Gal. 6:1-2; Matt. 5:5.

c. Matt. 5:7. "Blessed are the merciful, for they shall obtain mercy."
Cf. Luke 6:36.

d. Rom. 12:15-18. Rejoice with those who rejoice, weep with those who weep. Live in harmony with one another; do not be haughty, but associate with the lowly; never be conceited. Repay no one evil for evil, but take thought for what is noble in the sight of all. If possible, so far as it depends upon you, live peaceably with all.

e. Matt. 5:45. "Be sons of your Father who is in heaven; for he makes his sun rise on the evil and on the good, and sends rain on the just and on the unjust."

f. Matt. 5:44. "I say to you, Love your enemies and pray for those who persecute you."
Rom. 12:20-21. It is written, "If your enemy is hungry, feed him; if he is thirsty, give him drink; for by so doing you will heap burning coals upon his head." Do not be overcome by evil, but overcome evil with good.

LORD'S DAY 41

❶ QUESTION 108. *What does the seventh commandment teach us?*

That all unchastity is condemned by God,[a] and that we should therefore detest it from the heart,[b] and live chaste and disciplined lives,[c] whether in holy wedlock or in single life.[d]

a. Gal. 5:19-21. The works of the flesh are plain: immorality, impurity, licentiousness. . . . I warn you, as I warned you before, that those who do such things shall not inherit the kingdom of God.

b. Jude 23. Save some, by snatching them out of the fire; on some have mercy with fear, hating even the garment spotted by the flesh.

c. 1 Thess. 4:3-4. This is the will of God, that you should be holy: you must abstain from fornication; each one of you must learn to gain mastery over his body, to hallow and honor it (N.E.B.) .

d. Heb. 13:4. Let marriage be held in honor among all, and let the marriage bed be undefiled; for God will judge the immoral and adulterous.
Cf. 1 Cor. 7:1-9, 25-28.

℃ QUESTION 109. *Does God forbid nothing more than adultery and such gross sins in this commandment?*

Since both our body and soul are a temple of the Holy Spirit, it is his will that we keep both pure and holy. Therefore he forbids all unchaste actions, gestures, words,[a] thoughts, desires,[b] and whatever may excite another person to them.[c]

a. Eph. 5:3-4. Fornication and indecency of any kind, or ruthless greed, must not be so much as mentioned among you, as befits the people of God. No coarse, stupid, or flippant talk; these things are out of place; you should rather be thanking God (N.E.B.) .

Cf. 1 Cor. 6:18-20.

b. Matt. 5:27-29. "You have heard that it was said, 'You shall not commit adultery.' But I say to you that everyone who looks at a woman lustfully has already committed adultery with her in his heart. If your right eye causes you to sin, pluck it out and throw it away; it is better that you lose one of your members than that your whole body be thrown into hell."

c. Eph. 5:18. Do not get drunk with wine, for that is debauchery; but be filled with the Spirit.

Cf. 1 Cor. 15:33.

◖ QUESTION 110. *What does God forbid in the eighth commandment?*

He forbids not only the theft and robbery[a] which civil authorities punish, but God also labels as theft all wicked tricks and schemes by which we seek to get for ourselves our neighbor's goods, whether by force or under the pretext of right,[b] such as false weights[c] and measures,[d] deceptive advertising or merchandising,[e] counterfeit money, exorbitant interest,[f] or any other means forbidden by God. He also forbids all greed[g] and misuse and waste of his gifts.[h]

a. 1 Cor. 6:10. Nor thieves, nor the greedy, nor

drunkards, nor revilers, nor robbers will inherit the kingdom of God.

Cf. 1 Cor. 5:9-13.

b. Luke 3:14. Soldiers also asked him, "And we, what shall we do?" And he said to them, "Rob no one by violence or by false accusation, and be content with your wages."

Cf. 1 Thess. 4:6.

c. Prov. 11:1. A false balance is an abomination to the Lord, but a just weight is his delight.

d. Ezek. 45:10. "You shall have just balances, a just ephah, and a just bath."

Cf. Deut. 25:13-16.

e. Prov. 12:22. Lying lips are an abomination to the Lord, but those who act faithfully are his delight.

f. Luke 6:35. "Love your enemies, and do good, and lend, expecting nothing in return; and your reward will be great, and you will be sons of the Most High; for he is kind to the ungrateful and the selfish."

Cf. Ps. 15:5.

g. Luke 12:15. He said to them, "Take heed, and beware of all covetousness; for a man's life does not consist in the abundance of his possessions."

Cf. 1 Cor. 6:10.

h. Luke 16:1-2. He also said to the disciples, "There was a rich man who had a steward, and charges were brought to him that this man was wasting his goods. And he called him and said to him, 'What is this that I hear about you? Turn in the account of your stewardship, for you can no longer be steward.'"

❦ QUESTION 111. *But what does God require of you in this commandment?*

That I work for the good of my neighbor wherever I can and may, deal with him as I would have others deal with me,[a] and do my work well so that I may be able to help the poor in their need.[b]

a. Matt. 7:12: "Whatever you wish that men would do to you, do so to them; for this is the law and the prophets."
b. Eph. 4:28. Let the thief no longer steal, but rather let him labor, doing honest work with his hands, so that he may be able to give to those in need. Cf. Phil. 2:4.

❦ QUESTION 112. *What is required in the ninth commandment?*

That I do not bear false witness against anyone,[a] twist anyone's words,[b] be a gossip or a slanderer,[c] or condemn anyone lightly without a hearing.[d] Rather I am required to avoid, under penalty of God's wrath, all lying and deceit as the works of the devil himself.[e] In judicial and all other matters I am to love the truth, and to speak and confess it honestly.[f] Indeed, insofar as I am able, I am to defend and promote my neighbor's good name.[g]

a. Prov. 19:5. A false witness will not go unpunished, and he who utters lies will not escape.

b. Ps. 15:3, 5. [He] who does not slander with his tongue, and does no evil to his friend, nor takes up a reproach against his neighbor . . . shall never be moved.

c. Rom. 1:29-30. They were filled with all manner of wickedness, evil, covetousness, malice. Full of envy, murder, strife, deceit, malignity, they are gossips, slanderers, haters of God, insolent, haughty, boastful, inventors of evil, disobedient to parents.

d. Matt. 7:1. "Judge not, that you be not judged." Cf. Luke 6:37.

e. John 8:44. "You are of your father the devil, and your will is to do your father's desires. He was a murderer from the beginning, and has nothing to do with the truth, because there is no truth in him. When he lies, he speaks according to his own nature, for he is a liar and the father of lies."
Prov. 12:22; 13:5. Lying lips are an abomination to the Lord, but those who act faithfully are his delight. . . . A righteous man hates falsehood, but a wicked man acts shamefully and disgracefully. Cf. Lev. 19:11-12.

f. Eph. 4:25. Putting away falsehood, let everyone speak the truth with his neighbor, for we are members one of another.
Cf. 1 Cor. 13:6.

g. 1 Peter 4:8. Hold unfailing your love for one another, since love covers a multitude of sins.

❦ QUESTION 113. *What is required in the tenth commandment?*

That there should never enter our heart even the least inclination or thought contrary to any commandment of God, but that we should always hate sin with our whole heart and find satisfaction and joy in all righteousness.[a]

a. Rom. 7:7. What then shall we say? That the law is sin? By no means! Yet, if it had not been for the law, I should not have known sin. I should not have known what it is to covet if the law had not said, "You shall not covet."

❦ QUESTION 114. *But can those who are converted to God keep these commandments perfectly?*

No, for even the holiest of them make only a small beginning in obedience in this life.[a] Nevertheless, they begin with serious purpose to conform not only to some, but to all the commandments of God.[b]

a. 1 John 1:8. If we say we have no sin, we deceive ourselves, and the truth is not in us.
   Rom. 7:14. We know that the law is spiritual; but I am carnal, sold under sin.

b. Rom. 7:22. I delight in the law of God, in my inmost self.

James 2:10. Whoever keeps the whole law but fails in one point has become guilty of all of it.

❡ QUESTION 115. *Why, then, does God have the ten commandments preached so strictly since no one can keep them in this life?*

First, that all our life long we may become increasingly aware of our sinfulness,[a] and therefore more eagerly seek forgiveness of sins and righteousness in Christ.[b] Second, that we may constantly and diligently pray to God for the grace of the Holy Spirit, so that more and more we may be renewed in the image of God, until we attain the goal of full perfection after this life.[c]

a. 1 John 1:9. If we confess our sins, [God] is faithful and just, and will forgive our sins and cleanse us from all unrighteousness.

Cf. Ps. 32:5; Rom. 3:19; 7:7.

b. Rom. 7:24-25. Wretched man that I am! Who will deliver me from this body of death? Thanks be to God through Jesus Christ our Lord!

c. 1 Cor. 9:24. Do you not know that in a race all the runners compete, but only one receives the prize? So run that you may obtain it.

Cf. Phil. 3:12-14.

❡ QUESTION 116. *Why is prayer necessary for Christians?*

Because it is the chief part of the gratitude which God requires of us,[a] and because God will give his grace and Holy Spirit only to those who sincerely beseech him in prayer without ceasing, and who thank him for these gifts.[b]

a. Ps. 50:14-15. Offer to God a sacrifice of thanksgiving, and pay your vows to the Most High; and call upon me in the day of trouble; I will deliver you, and you shall glorify me.

b. Matt. 7:7-8. "Ask, and it will be given you; seek and you will find; knock, and it will be opened to you. For everyone who asks receives, and he who seeks finds, and to him who knocks it will be opened."
Cf. Luke 11:9-13.

❡ QUESTION 117. *What is contained in a prayer which pleases God and is heard by him?*

First, that we sincerely call upon the one true God, who has revealed himself to us in his Word,[a] for all that he has commanded us to ask of him.[b] Then, that we thoroughly acknowledge our need and evil condition[c] so that we may humble ourselves in the presence of his majesty.[d] Third, that we rest assured[e] that, in spite of our unworthiness, he will certainly hear our prayer for the sake of Christ our Lord, as he has promised us in his Word.[f]

a. Ps. 145:18. The Lord is near to all who call upon him, to all who call upon him in truth.
John 4:24. "God is Spirit, and those who worship him must worship in spirit and truth."

b. 1 John 5:14. This is the confidence which we have in [the Son of God], that if we ask anything according to his will he hears us.
Cf. James 1:5; Rom. 8:26.

c. Isa. 66:2. "All these things my hand has made, and so all these things are mine, says the Lord. But this is the man to whom I will look, he that is humble and contrite in spirit, and trembles at my word."
Cf. 2 Chron. 20:12.

d. 2 Chron. 7:14. "If my people who are called by my name humble themselves, and pray and seek my face, and turn from their wicked ways, then I will hear from heaven, and will forgive their sin and heal their land."

e. James 1:6. Let him ask in faith, with no doubting, for he who doubts is like a wave of the sea that is driven and tossed by the wind.

f. Matt. 7:8. "Everyone who asks receives, and he who seeks finds, and to him who knocks it will be opened."
John 14:13-14. "Whatever you ask in my name, I will do it, that the Father may be glorified in the

Son; if you ask anything in my name, I will do it."
Cf. Dan. 9:17-18; Rom. 10:13.

❡ QUESTION 118. *What has God commanded us to ask of him?*

All things necessary for soul and body[a] which Christ the Lord has included in the prayer which he himself taught us.

a. James 1:17. Every good endowment and every perfect gift is from above, coming down from the Father of lights with whom there is no variation or shadow due to change.

Matt. 6:33. Seek first [your heavenly Father's] kingdom and his righteousness, and all these things shall be yours as well.

❡ QUESTION 119. *What is the Lord's Prayer?*

"OUR FATHER WHO ART IN HEAVEN, HALLOWED BE THY NAME. THY KINGDOM COME, THY WILL BE DONE, ON EARTH AS IT IS IN HEAVEN. GIVE US THIS DAY OUR DAILY BREAD; AND FORGIVE US OUR DEBTS, AS WE ALSO HAVE FORGIVEN OUR DEBTORS; AND LEAD US NOT INTO TEMPTATION, BUT DELIVER US FROM EVIL, FOR THINE IS THE KINGDOM AND THE POWER AND THE GLORY, FOREVER.   AMEN."[a]

a. Matt. 6:9-13.
   Cf. Luke 11:2-4.

LORD'S DAY 46

❡ QUESTION 120.   *Why has Christ commanded us to address God: "Our Father"?*

That at the very beginning of our prayer he may awaken in us the childlike reverence and trust toward God which should be the motivation of our prayer, which is that God has become our Father through Christ and will much less deny us what we ask him in faith than our human fathers will refuse us earthly things.[a]

a. Matt. 7:9-11. "What man of you, if his son asks him for a loaf, will give him a stone? Or if he asks for a fish, will give him a serpent? If you then who are evil, know how to give good gifts to your children, how much more will your Father who is in heaven give good things to those who ask him?" Cf. Luke 11:11-13.

❡ QUESTION 121.   *Why is there added: "who art in heaven"?*

That we may have no earthly conception of the heavenly majesty of God,[a] but that we may expect from his almighty power all things that are needed for body and soul.[b]

a. Jer. 23:23-24. "Am I a God at hand, says the Lord, and not a God afar off? Can a man hide himself in secret places so that I cannot see him? says the

Lord. Do I not fill heaven and earth? says the Lord."

Cf. Acts 17:24-25.

b. Rom. 8:32. He who did not spare his own Son but gave him up for us all, will he not also give us all things with him?

Cf. Rom. 10:12.

❦ QUESTION 122. *What is the first petition?*

"Hallowed be thy name." That is: help us first of all to know thee rightly,[a] and to hallow, glorify, and praise thee in all thy works through which there shine thine almighty power, wisdom, goodness, righteousness, mercy, and truth.[b] And so order our whole life in thought, word, and deed that thy name may never be blasphemed on our account, but may always be honored and praised.[c]

a. John 17:3. "This is eternal life, that they know thee the only true God, and Jesus Christ whom thou hast sent."

Cf. Jer. 9:23-24; Matt. 16:17; Ps. 119:105; James 1:5.

b. Ps. 119:137. Righteous art thou, O Lord, and right are thy judgments.

Cf. Rom. 11:33-36.

c. Pss. 71:8; 115:1. My mouth is filled with thy praise, and with thy glory all the day. . . . Not to us, O Lord, not to us, but to thy name give glory, for the sake of thy steadfast love and thy faithfulness!

❡ QUESTION 123. *What is the second petition?*

"Thy kingdom come." That is: so govern us by thy Word and Spirit that we may more and more submit ourselves unto thee.[a] Uphold and increase thy church.[b] Destroy the works of the devil, every power that raises itself against thee, and all wicked schemes thought up against thy holy Word,[c] until the full coming of thy kingdom[d] in which thou shalt be all in all.[e]

a. Matt. 6:33. "Seek first [your heavenly Father's] kingdom and his righteousness, and all these things shall be yours as well."

Ps. 119:5. O that my ways may be steadfast in keeping thy statutes!

b. Ps. 51:18. Do good to Zion in thy good pleasure; rebuild the walls of Jerusalem.

c. 1 John 3:8. He who commits sin is of the devil; for the devil has sinned from the beginning. The reason the Son of God appeared was to destroy the works of the devil.

Cf. Rom. 16:20.

d. Rev. 22:17. The Spirit and the Bride say, "Come." And let him who hears say, "Come." And let him who is thirsty come, let him who desires take the water of life without price.

Cf. Rom. 8:22-24.

e. 1 Cor. 15:20, 28. In fact Christ has been raised from the dead, the first fruits of those who have fallen asleep. . . . When all things are subjected to him, then the Son himself will also be subjected to him who put all things under him, that God may be everything to everyone.

❡ QUESTION 124. *What is the third petition?*

"Thy will be done, on earth, as it is in heaven." That is: grant that we and all men may renounce our own will[a] and obey thy will, which alone is good, without grumbling,[b] so that everyone may carry out his office and calling as willingly and faithfully[c] as the angels in heaven.[d]

a. Matt. 16:24. Jesus told his disciples, "If any man would come after me, let him deny himself and take up his cross and follow me."
   Cf. Titus 2:12.
b. Luke 22:42. "Father, if thou art willing, remove this cup from me; nevertheless not my will, but thine, be done."
   Cf. Rom. 12:2; Eph. 5:10.
c. 1 Cor. 7:24. Brethren, in whatever state each was called, there let him remain with God.
d. Ps. 103:20. Bless the Lord, O you his angels, you mighty ones who do his word, hearkening to the voice of his word!

❡ QUESTION 125.   *What is the fourth petition?*

"Give us this day our daily bread." That is: be pleased to provide for all our bodily needs[a] so that thereby we may acknowledge that thou art the only source of all that is good,[b] and that without thy blessing neither our care and labor nor thy gifts can do us any good.[c] Therefore, may we withdraw our trust from all creatures and place it in thee alone.[d]

a. Ps. 104:27-28. These all look to thee, to give them their food in due season. When thou givest to them, they gather it up; when thou openest thy hand, they are filled with good things.
    Cf. Matt. 6:25-34.
b. Acts 14:17. "He did not leave himself without witness, for he did good and gave you from heaven rains and fruitful seasons, satisfying your hearts with food and gladness."
    Cf. Acts 17:25.
c. 1 Cor. 15:58. My beloved brethren, be steadfast, immovable, always abounding in the work of the Lord, knowing that in the Lord your labor is not in vain.
    Cf. Deut. 8:3; Pss. 37:3-11, 16-17; 127:1-2.
d. Ps. 55:22. Cast your burden on the Lord, and he will sustain you; he will never permit the righteous to be moved.
    Cf. Pss. 62:8, 10; 146:3.

❡ QUESTION 126. *What is the fifth petition?*

"And forgive us our debts, as we also have forgiven our debtors." That is: be pleased, for the sake of Christ's blood, not to charge to us, miserable sinners, our many transgressions, nor the evil which still clings to us.[a] We also find this witness of thy grace in us, that it is our sincere intention heartily to forgive our neighbor.[b]

a. 1 John 2:1-2. My little children, I am writing this to you so that you may not sin; but if anyone does sin, we have an advocate with the Father, Jesus Christ the righteous; and he is the expiation for our sins, and not for ours only but also for the sins of the whole world.
    Cf. Ps. 51:1-7.
b. Matt. 6:14-15. If you forgive men their trespasses, your heavenly Father also will forgive you; but if you do not forgive men their trespasses, neither will your Father forgive your trespasses.

❡ QUESTION 127. *What is the sixth petition?*

"And lead us not into temptation, but deliver us from evil." That is: since we are so weak that we cannot stand by ourselves for one moment,[a] and besides, since our sworn enemies, the devil,[b] the world,[c] and our own sin,[d] ceaselessly assail us, be pleased to preserve and strengthen us through the power of thy Holy Spirit so that we may stand firm against them, and not be defeated in this spiritual warfare,[e] until at last we obtain complete victory.[f]

a. John 15:5. "Apart from me you can do nothing." Cf. Ps. 103:14; Rom. 8:26.

b. 1 Peter 5:8. Be sober, be watchful. Your adversary the devil prowls around like a roaring lion, seeking someone to devour.

c. John 15:19. "If you were of the world, the world would love its own; but because you are not of the world, but I chose you out of the world, therefore the world hates you."
Cf. Eph. 6:12.

d. Rom. 7:23. I see in my members another law at war with the law of my mind and making me captive to the law of sin which dwells in my members.
Cf. Gal. 5:17.

e. Matt. 26:41. "Watch and pray that you may not enter into temptation; the spirit indeed is willing, but the flesh is weak."
Cf. Mark 13:33.

f. 1 Thess. 3:13; 5:23. [May he] establish your hearts unblamable in holiness before our God and Father, at the coming of our Lord Jesus with all his saints. . . . May the God of peace himself sanctify you wholly; and may your spirit and soul and body be kept sound and blameless at the coming of our Lord Jesus Christ.

❡ QUESTION 128. *How do you close this prayer?*

"For thine is the kingdom and the power and the glory, forever." That is: we ask all this of thee because, as our King, thou art willing and able to give us all that is good since thou hast power over all things,[a] and that by this not we ourselves but thy holy name may be glorified forever.[b]

a. Rom. 10:12-13. There is no distinction between Jew and Greek; the same Lord is Lord of all and bestows his riches upon all who call upon him. For, "everyone who calls upon the name of the Lord will be saved."
Cf. 2 Peter 2:9.
b. John 14:13. "Whatever you ask in my name, I will do it, that the Father may be glorified in the Son."
Cf. Ps. 115:1.

❡ QUESTION 129. *What is the meaning of the little word "Amen"?*

Amen means: this shall truly and certainly be. For my prayer is much more certainly heard by God than I am persuaded in my heart that I desire such things from him.[a]

a. 2 Cor. 1:20. All the promises of God find their Yes in him. That is why we utter the Amen through him, to the glory of God.

2 Tim. 2:13. If we are faithless, he remains faithful
—for he cannot deny himself.

Isa. 65:24. "Before they call I will answer, while
they are yet speaking I will hear," says the Lord.
Cf. Jer. 28:6.